An American adviser (left) and two South Vietnamese soldiers are poled across a river. South Vietnam took on more responsibility for fighting the war after 1968.

WAR IN VIETNAM

Book III—Vietnamization
By David K. Wright

CHILDRENS PRESS ®

CHICAGO

U.S. troops prepare wounded soldiers for medical evacuation. American military deaths and injuries helped influence the way people in the United States felt about this increasingly unpopular war.

Library of Congress Cataloging-in-Publication Data

Wright, David K.
  War in Vietnam. (Vietnamization) / by David K. Wright.
    p.   cm.
  Includes index.
  Summary: Follows the conflict in Vietnam from the period of intensification at the time of Richard Nixon's election to its conclusion and the withdrawal of American troops.
  ISBN 0-516-02288-1
    1. Vietnamese Conflict, 1961-1975—Juvenile literature. [1. Vietnamese Conflict, 1961-1975.] I. Title. II. Title: Vietnamization.
DS557.7.W74   1988   88-14981
959.704'3—dc19   CIP
                                           AC

Childrens Press®, Chicago
Copyright ©1989 by Regensteiner Publishing Enterprises, Inc.
All rights reserved. Published simultaneously in Canada.
Printed in the United States of America.
1 2 3 4 5 6 7 8 9 10 R 97 96 95 94 93 92 91 90 89 88

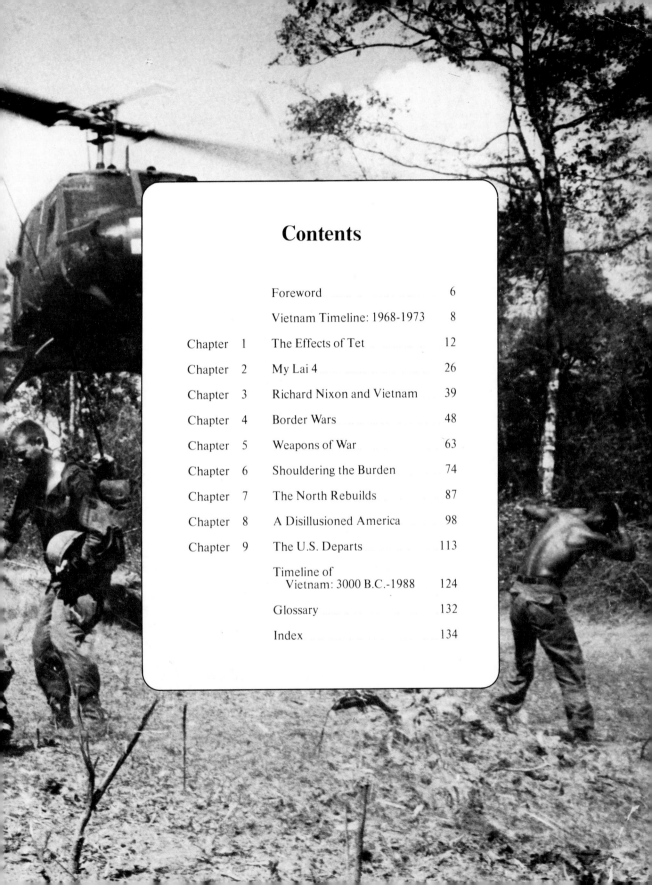

Contents

Foreword

Vietnam. The land, the war, the experience continue to haunt the nation. It was the first war America lost, and lost causes always seem to leave more questions than answers. The four-volume series *War in Vietnam* by David K. Wright looks at why the United States became involved, why we fought the war the way we did, and why we lost. In seeking answers to these questions, Mr. Wright contributes to the healing of the nation, which remains the unfinished business of the war.

In Book I—*Eve of Battle*, Wright describes the early history of Vietnam up to the critical year 1965, when the first U. S. combat troops arrived in South Vietnam. We learn of Vietnam's long tradition of fierce independence, the period of French rule over the country, the first French-Indochina war involving the nationalist Viet Minh, and the growing American involvement following the French defeat in 1954. Wright shows us how America's entanglement deepened step by step. By 1965 the leaders in Washington, D. C., felt they had no choice but to send U. S. combat troops to save Vietnam from communism. *Eve of Battle* reveals the danger of making important national decisions without really understanding the nature and history of the people we have pledged to support.

Book II—*A Wider War* explores one of the most puzzling questions of the conflict. Why couldn't the United States—the world's greatest military power—defeat a poorly equipped peasant army? Some argue that America's politicians would not use the military force necessary to win. But *A Wider War* shows that the amount of force Americans used was much greater than in any other war. Such firepower and violence—from the smallest infantry unit to the giant B-52 bombers—turned the Vietnamese peasants against the U. S. It turned many Americans against the war as well. To these people, including some Vietnam veterans, it appeared that time was on the enemy's side. Before long, many in America lost patience with this long, costly, and savage war.

Book III—*Vietnamization* tells of the events that followed the 1968 election of Richard Nixon as President. Even though Nixon had pledged to seek "peace with honor," he pursued a complex and at times dishonest policy in running the war. In violation of the law, Nixon ordered U.S. troops to invade Cambodia and Laos. We also learn how he promised to reduce the number of U. S. troops in Vietnam yet still increase support for the South Vietnamese Army. He stepped up the bombing of North Vietnam at the same time he began secret talks with the enemy in Paris. This book also wrestles with the agonizing question of how American soldiers could have taken part in the March 1968 massacre of innocent Vietnamese civilians. The My Lai 4 incident, in which hundreds of men, women, and children were murdered, remains a black mark against America's honor. The book concludes with the heavy Christmas bombing of North Vietnam in December 1972 and with the January 1973 cease-fire agreement. The treaty ended American involvement in Vietnam but did not end the war.

The final book — *The Fall of Vietnam* — recounts the tragic consequences of America's confused policies in Vietnam. In our efforts to bring democracy and freedom to this far-away nation, we nearly lost sight of these values at home. The Watergate political scandal showed that even President Nixon and his close advisers were willing to break the law to stay in power. Richard Nixon became the only President in history forced to resign in disgrace. In one sense he can be counted as a victim of Vietnam. More tragic victims were the populations of North and South Vietnam, Cambodia, and Laos. Many U. S. Vietnam veterans also remain troubled victims of the war. No one can predict when the agony will end for the families of MIAs — those reported missing in action from 1965 to 1973. These families have waited for years to hear some word about the fate of their loved ones.

Vietnam is a sad chapter in the nation's history. The series *War in Vietnam* will help readers find answers to many of their questions about the war. The biggest question of all may be — Was Vietnam an isolated, regrettable event, or did our conduct of the war reveal the darker side of the American character? The answer to this question, perhaps more than any other, has meaning for the nation's future.

Frank A. Burdick
Professor of History at
State University College
Cortland, New York

A Vietnam Timeline: Major Events in Vietnamization

1968

January 30-31: The largest enemy attack of the war begins on the first day of Tet, the Oriental new year holiday.

February 24: South Vietnamese retake the Imperial Palace in Hué.

March 10: *The New York Times* reports that General William Westmoreland wants 206,000 more American troops by the end of the year.

March 12: Eugene McCarthy, the antiwar U.S. senator from Minnesota, receives 40 percent of the Democratic vote in the New Hampshire presidential primary.

March 16: Between 200 and 600 Vietnamese civilians are murdered by American troops in a remote village called My Lai 4.

March 31: President Lyndon B. Johnson orders a halt to the bombing of North Vietnam and announces that he will not run again for the presidency.

April 4: Dr. Martin Luther King, Jr., is shot to death in Memphis,

American Marines amid the rubble of Hué during the 1968 Tet Offensive.

Tennessee. Rioting erupts in many large U.S. cities.

May 11: Formal peace talks begin in Paris between the United States and North Vietnam.

June 6: U.S. Senator Robert Kennedy dies the day after he is shot in Los Angeles, California. Kennedy had been campaigning for the Democratic presidential nomination.

June 10: General Creighton Abrams takes command of U.S. forces in Vietnam.

June 27: American troops leave Khe Sanh after several months of bitter fighting.

July 1: U.S. planes resume heavy bombing north of the DMZ.

August 8: Richard M. Nixon is nominated by Republicans to run for the presidency.

August 26-29: Vice President Hubert Humphrey receives the nomination for the presidency in Chicago as police and antiwar demonstrators clash violently in the city's streets.

Richard M. Nixon on the campaign trail, 1968.

November 6:	Richard M. Nixon is elected President.
December 31:	A total of 540,000 Americans are in South Vietnam.

1969

March 18:	The secret bombing of Cambodia begins.
March 28:	U.S. and ARVN troops discover mass graves of civilians killed by Viet Cong and NVA during the Tet takeover of Hué.
June 8:	President Nixon announces that 25,000 American troops will be withdrawn and replaced by South Vietnamese forces.
September 3:	Ailing Ho Chi Minh dies in Hanoi at the age of 79.
Fall:	Huge antiwar rallies take place in Washington, D.C.
November 16:	The country learns of the tragic massacre in My Lai 4.
December 31:	The number of U.S. troops in Vietnam drops to 480,000.

1970

February 20:	Henry Kissinger and Le Duc Tho of North

Antiwar activists perch on a Washington, D.C., peace monument during a rally against U.S. policy in Southeast Asia.

Vietnam meet secretly in Paris to discuss a possible cease-fire.

March 18: Prince Sihanouk of Cambodia is overthrown by Cambodian military officers.

April 30: American and South Vietnamese forces invade Cambodia.

May 4: National Guardsmen kill 4 antiwar students and wound 11 others at Kent State University in Ohio.

December 31: The number of U.S. troops in Vietnam falls to 280,000.

1971

January 6: Congress repeals the Gulf of Tonkin Resolution.

February 8: South Vietnamese forces enter Laos in an attempt to cut the Ho Chi Minh Trail.

March 29: Lieutenant William Calley is convicted of murder in connection with the massacre at My Lai 4.

December 31: U.S. forces now total 140,000.

1972

May 8: President Nixon mines the main North

Le Duc Tho (left) of North Vietnam and Henry Kissinger.

Vietnamese harbor and steps up the bombing.

June 17: A night watchman catches five men attempting to break into Democratic national headquarters at the Watergate apartments in Washington, D.C.

November 7: Richard Nixon is re-elected President.

December 31: U.S. combat troops number fewer than 30,000.

1973

January 27: Kissinger signs a peace agreement with the North Vietnamese in Paris.

March 29: The last U.S. combat troops leave Vietnam.

Chapter 1

The Effects of Tet

The United States kept score in the Vietnam War by counting bodies. If ten enemy soldiers died in a firefight and only one American or South Vietnamese was killed, the U.S. believed it was winning the war. Americans did not realize that the Viet Cong and the North Vietnamese Army (NVA) were willing to accept very high casualties. In fact, no one in North Vietnam kept track of how many people died. It is estimated that about one million North Vietnamese lost their lives from 1965 to 1973. But they were quickly replaced from a population of 22 million that had a high birth rate.

Body counts haunted General William Westmoreland, the commander of American forces. His people at Military Assistance Command, Vietnam (MACV), headquarters ordered their officers to count the number of enemy their troops killed. Some American officers felt forced to make up numbers they knew were inaccurate. If an officer didn't have much of a body count, someone might think he wasn't doing his job. So when a soldier dropped a hand grenade in a tunnel, he would be asked to guess how many enemy were killed inside. This system was later to be the subject of a well-publicized lawsuit. CBS-TV accused Westmoreland of making up body counts, and the general sued the network in 1983 without success.

Unfortunately, the 1968 Tet Offensive (Tet is the lunar or Chinese new year) left many bodies to be counted. Americans and South Vietnamese suffered hundreds of casualties in what turned out to be one of the biggest enemy attacks of the war. For more than three weeks, fighting raged in major cities such as Saigon, Danang, and the old royal capital of Hué. In Hué, American and South Vietnamese forces

Weary Marines rest after a battle in Hué during the 1968 Tet Offensive.

President Lyndon B. Johnson announces that he will not seek re-election.

found the mass graves of 2,800 innocent civilians killed by the Viet Cong and North Vietnamese. Hué's people were independent, and many did not want to fight on either side in the war. The enemy believed Hué citizens supported the Saigon government and shot or clubbed or buried them alive while the NVA held the city. Once Hué was retaken, some South Vietnamese soldiers also killed civilians, believing they had supported the NVA. Hué's people learned that being neutral could be as terrifying as choosing a side.

The American public, siding with U.S. forces, found the fighting hard to watch each evening on television. All across the country, troubled Americans were saying: "But I thought we were *winning* the war!" Film footage made it seem the war was hanging in the balance. Stunned U.S. citizens began to criticize the way that the Johnson administration was running the conflict. Pressure on President Johnson became so great that he decided not to seek re-election in 1968.

Tet had other important effects:

• Westmoreland was replaced by General Creighton Abrams in June. Westmoreland left Vietnam still insisting that the U.S. and its allies had crushed the enemy. Yet he had asked for more troops

14

soon after Tet to mount another offensive against the VC.

• Secretary of Defense Robert McNamara, who had warned President Johnson that the war was not going well, was replaced by Clark Clifford.

• American antiwar groups used the Tet Offensive to recruit people who had not had strong opinions about the war. Some citizens saw Tet, along with drug use, sexual freedom, and inner-city unrest, as another sign that their country was unraveling. If America was in such trouble, they asked, shouldn't we first fix matters at home?

This discontent was an added bonus for the North Vietnamese and what was left of the Viet Cong. The NVA and Viet Cong had gambled that the Tet attacks would spark a general uprising in Vietnam. No such uprising took place. While in many areas the battles lasted for days, even weeks, there was little doubt that American and South Vietnamese troops would hold on. Yet, while Tet was not successful militarily, it dealt a psychological blow to American morale.

The influence of Tet showed clearly in American politics,

Eugene J. McCarthy

Eugene J. McCarthy (born March 29, 1916), former U.S. senator

Minnesotan Eugene McCarthy was a college economics and sociology teacher who won a seat in the U.S. House of Representatives. The Democrat later was elected to the Senate, where he became an early opponent of the war in Vietnam. When no one else showed the courage to oppose Lyndon Johnson early in 1968, McCarthy decided to run.

He was an instant favorite of college students, who left school for days at a time to campaign for him. McCarthy won 40 percent of the Democratic prima-ry vote in New Hampshire. The victory helped convince President Johnson not to seek another term. As an underdog, he continued to run until the Chicago politi-cal convention. There, his backers were beaten and his headquarters invaded by police.

A soft-spoken Catholic intellectual, McCarthy left the Senate in 1970. He has written 15 books on a range of topics from politics to poetry.

where a little-known antiwar sena-tor, Eugene J. McCarthy of Min-nesota, almost beat President

Johnson in the Democratic primary in New Hampshire. College students had cut their hair and pulled on fresh clothing to go door-to-door for peace in a "Stay clean for Gene" campaign. It worked well. Four days later, U.S. Senator Robert F. Kennedy of New York joined the presidential race. Lyndon Johnson, disliked by many Democrats for not handling the war as they wanted, had already announced on March 31 that he would not run for re-election. Instead, Vice President Hubert Humphrey would campaign for the Democratic nomination.

At the same time, President Johnson ordered a halt to the bombing of North Vietnam. He believed this might encourage the North Vietnamese to talk peace. In a way, this was a tougher decision than not running for office again. Johnson was under constant pressure from the military to intensify the bombing. He was under pressure from Congress and public leaders to halt the air war altogether. So he stopped bombing all of North Vietnam except around the demilitarized zone (DMZ), an area that marked the dividing line between North

and South Vietnam.

DMZ bombing was intended to pound the 40,000 North Vietnamese Army troops who surrounded Khe Sanh. This base was used by about 5,000 U.S. Marines, who had been ordered to disrupt enemy activity in the northwest corner of South Vietnam. Besides thousands of enemy soldiers all around them, the Marines were under constant fire from NVA artillery hidden in the surrounding hills. The harder the NVA tried to take Khe Sanh, the deeper the Marines dug in. Throughout the late winter and spring of 1968, artillery and waves of NVA soldiers tried to wipe out the base. The Marines held firm.

It was not easy. Patrols sent out each day were shot to pieces. Enemy fire was so heavy that the Marines could not get out of their trenches to bathe or brush their teeth. When supplies or ammunition were dropped from cargo planes, the soldiers ran through walls of shrapnel (exploding artillery or mortar fragments) to retrieve them. Body bags lay along the lone runway, waiting for any cargo plane that dared stop long enough to load the dead aboard.

A U.S. helicopter, in flames after being shot down by enemy fire, is doused by Marines in Khe Sanh.

Used to being on the attack, the Marines gritted their teeth and tried to stay sane.

America followed the blow-by-blow defense of Khe Sanh. To curb enemy guns, U.S. planes dropped the equivalent of five World War II atomic bombs on the surrounding hills. Thousands of NVA soldiers must have died in this area, which looked like the surface of the moon. Lyndon Johnson was so intent on keeping Khe Sanh open that he asked several high-ranking military men to sign pledges that the Americans would not be overrun.

Eventually, the North Vietnamese pulled back, and the Marines were relieved by South Vietnamese forces and by U.S. 1st Cavalry Division troops. The North Vietnamese may have wanted to score a victory similar to the one at Dien Bien Phu in 1954 over the French. Or, they may have felt that Marine patrols were disrupting their infiltration (entry into South Vietnam). Most likely, the siege was used to draw U.S. attention away from South Vietnam's cities so that the Tet Offensive could succeed.

General Vo Nguyen Giap, who had beaten the French at Dien Bien Phu in 1954, led the North Vietnamese at Khe Sanh. This battle showed that neither side was winning the war, but Giap felt the deadlock favored the communists. He suspected that relations between Saigon and Washington would become more strained as America pressured South Vietnam to do more of the fighting. Giap agreed with top North Vietnamese leaders that prolonging the war would increase the chances of a settlement favorable both to Hanoi and to the Viet Cong guerrillas.

Tet almost wiped out the Viet Cong, who had done much of the fighting on the communist side. Yet within weeks they were causing problems again. In late May, Saigon once more came under heavy attack.

The Johnson administration began peace talks in May that excluded both the VC and the Saigon government. South Viet-

Rev. Martin Luther King, Jr.

namese officials were resentful, even though U.S. negotiators Averell Harriman and Cyrus Vance told the North Vietnamese that America would not deal with the Viet Cong.

Meanwhile, events in the United States seemed just as chaotic. Civil rights leader Martin Luther King, Jr. was shot to death on April 4 in Memphis, Tennessee, by racist James Earl Ray. Rioting erupted in Baltimore, Detroit, and other cities following King's assassination. Ironically, Vietnam veterans were among those called out to help restore order. On June 6 presidential hopeful Robert Kennedy died in Los Angeles, one day after being shot by Sirhan B. Sirhan; the assassin hated Kennedy's stand on Middle East politics. Many Americans became more concerned with issues of law and order than with civil rights or the war in Vietnam.

Later that summer, national conventions were held to pick the 1968 presidential candidates. Former Vice President Richard M. Nixon was nominated by the Republicans. Alabama Governor George C. Wallace was the nominee of the newly formed Independent Party. To an increasing number of Americans tired of Lyndon Johnson, Nixon and Wallace seemed to offer hard-line alternatives to Johnson's con-

Robert F. Kennedy

Robert F. Kennedy (1925-1968), U.S. senator

The younger brother of President John F. Kennedy, Robert served as Attorney General in his brother's administration. He resigned after his brother was killed on November 22, 1963. Robert was never a close friend of Lyndon Johnson, but some of Johnson's advisors were close friends of Kennedy. One was Secretary of Defense Robert McNamara. He told Kennedy privately that he had second thoughts on the conduct of the war in Vietnam.

This helped shape Robert's views on the war, which were opposed to those of Johnson. After antiwar Senator Eugene McCarthy's strong showing in the New Hampshire primary election, Kennedy joined the 1968 presidential race.

For the next few months, all eyes turned to the Democratic primaries. Robert Kennedy was an effective campaigner and emerged as the party favorite. On the night of his June victory in the California primary, Kennedy was shot by a lone gunman, Sirhan Sirhan, and died the following day. Sirhan shot Kennedy because of the candidate's strong pro-Israeli position.

fused policies. Many antiwar protestors backed Senator Eugene McCarthy at the Democratic convention in Chicago. But the hard-line approach won there, too. Vice President Hubert H. Humphrey, who believed we could win in Vietnam, became the Democratic nominee.

Antiwar activists staged demonstrations in Chicago, where the Democratic convention was being held. Mayor Richard J. Daley's police force attacked protesters as television cameras recorded the brutal scene. Pacifists and activists alike were injured and arrested in what was later described as a police riot. The chaos was yet another tragedy played out live in 1968 as millions of viewers tuned in. Humphrey received the nomination but lost antiwar voters, who advocated sitting out the

Chicago police break up an antiwar rally during the 1968 Democratic convention.

Chicago Mayor Richard J. Daley denied charges that city police had "rioted."

Vice President Hubert H. Humphrey at a campaign stop. His nomination split the Democratic Party along war-versus-peace lines.

November election. Richard Nixon won the election, though Humphrey surged strongly at the end. Democrats also were abandoned by blue-collar voters, many of whom backed George Wallace.

Throughout this period, there was an air in the United States of choosing sides on a number of issues. McGeorge Bundy, a former Johnson advisor, told a college audience that he now backed a bombing halt and troop withdrawal. In San Francisco, 1,000 veterans and soldiers on active duty led a huge antiwar march. Popular music themes were filled with verses about confrontations between young and old and parents and children. One of the strengths of the antiwar movement was its youth. At the time, there was an unusually large number of Americans in high schools and colleges. They were automatically wary of anything older people supported, which included the war. "Never trust anyone over 30" became a national rallying cry for many.

Young people were influential elsewhere. In London, about 5,000 British antiwar activists staged a protest march. Swedes offered U.S. military men stationed in Germany a safe country in which to desert and live. Later, the Swedes gave North Vietnam economic assistance. Canadians permitted draft resisters to live in their country. Most large American cities had coffee houses and offices where persons about to be drafted could go for advice. These storefronts often helped draft resisters leave the country.

In Paris, where the aged but skillful Averell Harriman faced North Vietnamese representatives, there was little progress. To the anger and amazement of many, peace talks stalled over the size and shape of the table and where each delegate would sit! People on both sides were dying and the diplomats seemed to be toying with human lives. A poll at the end of 1968 showed that Vietnam was the world's most urgent concern among many people.

It should have been. Approximately 31,000 Americans had been killed by December 31, 1968. More than 200,000 had been wounded. Almost half a million North Vietnamese had died. Hundreds of thousands of South Vietnamese—including civilians

South Vietnamese women bought many black-market goods during the war.

caught in bombings or crossfire— had died as well. An even larger number of refugees crowded into cities. Most were simple country folk who did not know how to support themselves in over-crowded cities. They became whatever anyone wanted them to become: thieves, shoeshine boys, bartenders, or black marketeers.

A few persons worried about even deeper moral problems. The Geneva Convention was created in 1864 so that enemies could be treated humanely in time of war. It was disregarded by everyone in Vietnam. The VC had a long and

Vietnam veterans and peace activists protest the war. By the end of 1968, some 31,000 Americans had been killed in or near Vietnam. More than 200,000 had been wounded.

shameful history of killing villagers who disagreed with their politics. North Vietnam overran outposts, killing rather than capturing the defenders. The South Vietnamese openly tortured suspected VC in front of American soldiers. U.S. troops were not without blame, either.

Several weapons, banished by international agreement for use against ground forces, were employed by U.S. troops anyway. One was the 50-caliber machine gun, an automatic weapon whose bullets seemed as big as railroad spikes. Because the bullets ripped so much tissue when they hit, the 50-caliber was supposed to be used only against airplanes, tanks, and other armored vehicles. But the VC had none of these. Instead, U.S. forces used the 50s on the Viet Cong themselves. Not only were the 50s standard equipment on American tanks, there was also a special "Quad 50" truck that carried four 50-caliber weapons. It, too, was used on VC and NVA ground units.

As Richard Nixon took office in January 1969, there were few signs that the war was going to become more bearable.

Chapter 2

My Lai 4

In every war, each side believes that its citizens and soldiers are the "good guys" and that the enemy is more brutal and less human. When and if "our" soldiers commit brutal acts, ways are found to explain them.

But on March 16, 1968, something happened that defied explanation: Roughly 130 U.S. soldiers—ordinary young men who had been drafted into the Army—murdered between 200 and 600 South Vietnamese women, children, and old people in a village called My Lai 4.

The massacre was not uncovered until late 1969. Most Americans could not believe that it had happened. Despite evidence that included photographs, many considered it impossible that U.S. soldiers could commit such an atrocity. Not until the Pentagon launched a full investigation did America begin to ask a number of anguished questions. How could

the killings have happened? If the story was true, why did it take so long to be told? Was this an isolated incident, or had other massacres been committed by U.S. troops during the war?

As the investigation proceeded, eyewitnesses told their stories, and the tragic events of March 16 began to unfold. . . .

The soldiers were members of an infantry company in the U.S. Americal Division. After serving several months in Vietnam, they were told that they would be going on an important operation in a nearby village. The village was in South Vietnam's northernmost province, Quang Ngai, a longtime Viet Cong stronghold. The province was important to American and South Vietnamese forces because its northern border was the demilitarized zone. West of Quang Ngai was Khe Sanh, where U.S. Marines were under attack at the time by thousands of NVA

Sharpened wooden stakes in a pit, built to catch an unsuspecting U.S. or South Vietnamese soldier.

soldiers. Khe Sanh was considered a key target.

Company C or "Charlie" Company had trained in Hawaii before being sent to Vietnam. The men were young and not well educated, and many had been drafted. Had they enlisted, they might have chosen to be trained as supply clerks or typists. That decision would have meant spending three or four years in the Army instead of two. The men in Charlie Company were not people who took the initiative but who usually waited for something to happen and then reacted to it.

The company had been in the field looking for the enemy for some time. Instead of seeing many enemy soldiers, the Americans ran into a series of deadly booby traps. Some were no doubt set by civilians who supported the VC. In one case, however, a mine field that killed 6 members of the company and wounded 12 others was set by allies, Korean soldiers! The Koreans had put out the mines so they could sleep at night. But when the Koreans pulled out, they had forgotten to pick them up or to notify anyone that the mines were still there. Some

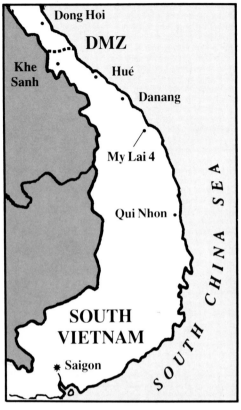

My Lai 4 is in northern South Vietnam, near Danang.

members of Charlie Company knew the mine field was active, but for reasons that aren't clear, the men walked into the area anyway and suffered 18 casualties.

The incident occurred in February 1968 just north of the village of My Lai 4. The angry soldiers blamed the villagers for some of the mines and booby traps that had killed and wounded members in their company. Their commander did nothing to discourage

Army Captain Ernest Medina was the company commander during the fateful operation in the village of My Lai 4 in March 1968.

the men's desire to get revenge.

The company commander, Captain Ernest Medina, had come out of a poor, small town in rural Colorado. Medina joined the Army, then became an officer as a way to better himself. He was eager to command troops in Vietnam because it would make up for his lack of education if he decided on a career in the military. Medina was aggressive and excelled at motivating his men. It is clear that he told them, just before they flew toward My Lai 4, that they would be fighting experienced and dangerous Viet Cong. Some troops heard Medina say to leave nothing alive in the village; others heard him say only to wipe out the Viet Cong. The men were eager to find an enemy who would stand and fight. One person who always listened to Captain Medina was a platoon leader, Lieutenant William L. Calley, Jr.

Lt. William Calley, Jr., leaves court after being convicted of murder.

Unlike the powerfully built, popular Medina, Calley was a short young man who had flunked out of junior college and had generally been unsuccessful at what he had tried. He was happy when the Army asked him to be an officer shortly after he joined. The young man became a second lieutenant upon graduation from officers' candidate school. At the age of 24, he found himself in charge of about 30 men—one of four platoons in Medina's company. Calley, unsure of himself, was anxious to please the more experienced captain.

From the start, Calley was at best indifferent and at worst cruel to the Vietnamese. Apparently, Medina set the example for Calley, and Calley set the example for the men in his platoon. One man in Charlie Company put it this way: "First, you'd stop the people, question them, and let them go. Second, you'd stop the people, beat up an old man, and let them go. Third, you'd stop the people, beat up an old man, then shoot him. Fourth, you'd go in and wipe out a village." Medina and Calley took part in and witnessed acts of brutality long before My Lai 4, soldiers later testified at the Army trial.

Gradually, during their time in Quang Ngai province, Calley and his platoon grew to hate all Vietnamese. They did not understand Vietnamese customs. Their fears were fed by stories of booby-trapped babies, broken glass in soft drinks sold by children, and mines and booby traps triggered by women and old people. The run-ins with the mines left by the Koreans fueled their anger. When the helicopters landed just outside My Lai 4 on the morning of March 16, the men jumped out and quickly started shooting. To their surprise, no one fired back. If the VC were in the area, they apparently did not want a fight.

Medina and Calley led Charlie Company into the village, where they began questioning villagers. What happened next was simple and horrible. One of the soldiers stabbed an old man, and as if a signal had been given, the young Americans started killing hundreds of people. It must have been strange — troops chasing and shooting young and old Vietnamese as the noise from small arms fire and the haze and smell

Civilian deaths occurred all over South Vietnam throughout the war.

of gunpowder hung in the hot, damp air. The soldiers tossed hand grenades into huts where families were trying to hide. They killed all the animals, stabbing several cattle repeatedly with bayonets. Lieutenant Calley and Captain Medina, by several different accounts, were in the thick of the action.

At one point Calley herded about 100 civilians into a ditch that ran parallel to the village. While the people huddled under the hot sun, Calley and several soldiers turned their M-16 rifles on automatic. They emptied dozens of 17-shot clips into the crying villagers. After a great deal of firing, they walked along the ditch and shot whoever moved. The only people who escaped death at My Lai 4 were those who ran out of the village and a few who somehow survived gunshot and fragmentation wounds.

Yet even in this incredible waste of human life, there was a hero. A helicopter pilot, Hugh Thompson, saw the dead in the ditch and landed in an attempt to help them. He was too late. Returning to his helicopter, he then spotted a group of women

Chief Warrant Officer
Hugh C. Thompson.

and children huddled not far from the ditch. Several of Calley's men also had seen the group and began to move toward them. Thompson ordered his door gunner to aim the gunner's M-60 machine gun at Calley's men and to shoot them if they tried to kill the Vietnamese. Thompson then hurried the group of civilians on board his helicopter and flew off with them. He was later awarded a medal for his heroic rescue.

Helicopter radio messages made the operation in My Lai 4 sound as if a massacre had occurred.

Not everyone on the ground took part in the killing. One soldier shot himself in the foot, perhaps to avoid having to kill a civilian. A reporter and a photographer for the American Division newspaper recorded the entire event on black-and-white and color film. Neither had much combat experience, but both believed they had witnessed a massacre. It was impossible to tell how many people died. Several different sources indicated later that the number was above 500.

When Medina's company returned to base they were credited with killing 128 Viet Cong. Yet the captain's report contained some odd discrepancies. If that many VC had been killed, then where were the enemy weapons? Only three rifles had been captured from My Lai 4. Also, how was it possible to kill 128 enemy soldiers and suffer only one casualty—a self-inflicted gunshot wound? An American Division officer at the base had tape-recorded radio messages received and sent during the My Lai 4 operation. When he played the tape back repeatedly, it sounded to him as if helicopter crews were seeing a mass killing of civilians by U.S. ground forces. No one followed up on these questions, however, and gradually, the terrible events of March 16, 1968, faded away.

My Lai 4 stayed alive in the mind of a helicopter door gunner named Ron Ridenhour. He had seen some of the violence and knew it was wrong. But he suspected the Army would cover up the massacre. He feared someone might kill him if he drew attention to it while still in the service.

Ridenhour was discharged in December 1968. Once back in Arizona, he began to write to various congressmen and military officials about the killings at My Lai 4. Eventually, Senator Morris Udall of Arizona believed him. The Pentagon began an investigation, but so slowly that Ridenhour finally took his story to the press. The public learned the truth about the massacre in November 1969. Soldiers who had been at My Lai 4 quickly confirmed what had happened.

Medina and Calley were arrested and held for military trial. The lieutenant was accused of killing 109 "Oriental civilians." Medina and four others were accused of murder and the torture of a VC suspect. By March 1970, a total of 14 officers were charged with covering up the massacre. Everyone on trial entered pleas of

Ron Ridenhour.

innocent. Of all those accused of crimes, only Calley was convicted. There was not enough evidence to convict the others. Calley's awards and decorations were taken away from him. On March 29, he was found guilty of killing 22 civilians. His life term later was reduced to 20 years in prison, and he was paroled in 1974.

Helicopters could drop hundreds of soldiers into an area in a few minutes.

In the military and among supporters of the war, there were two reactions. First, they refused to believe that U.S. troops killed anyone except the enemy. When proof indicated otherwise, they moved to back those officers and enlisted men who were accused of the crimes. Many Americans, those who supported the war and those who opposed it, were shocked at Calley's sentence. They felt that he was "taking the rap" for officers above him. Calley probably never realized the impact of what he had done at My Lai 4. In fact, a national magazine paid him to pose for its annual Christmas cover amidst a number of babies!

Long after Calley's court martial trial, Americans asked themselves how such a thing could have happened. The military pointed out that student deferments for college-age men had forced the Army to lower its standards. Under normal conditions, Calley would never have been an officer. The deferments also caused the military to "recycle" young men who were not quite intelligent enough to pass tests for induction. At least a dozen of these disadvantaged people were in Medina's infantry company.

Intelligent or not, U.S. soldiers did not know much about the Vietnamese. It made no sense to the average American that someone who couldn't read or didn't own a car could have a complicated culture. Soldiers received only a few hours of information about Vietnamese. But such a lecture was sometimes given by a sergeant who had never been in a local village. A wallet-sized card telling soldiers how to treat prisoners often was stuck in a pocket and forgotten.

Obviously, such an event as My Lai 4 did not encourage student draftees to become officers. In fact, it did just the opposite. An increasing number of college graduates who were drafted into the Army took their chances for two years and then left the military. A few of the young officers who remained were graduates of military academies (who could be kept in the military indefinitely in time of war). Most were people like Medina who wanted to better themselves. One former soldier recalls: "We had a first lieutenant from Boston whose only job before the Army was wiping off seats at ballgames in Fenway Park. Is that the kind of guy you want to lead you into battle?"

The My Lai 4 tragedy added to the strain under which U.S. troops operated.

Chapter 3

Richard Nixon and Vietnam

In many ways, it made sense that Richard Nixon was elected President of the United States in 1968. Even though there were more Democrats than Republicans in the country at that time, many people in both parties were angry at President Lyndon Johnson and at the Democratic nominee, Vice President Hubert Humphrey. Democrats who wanted to win the war thought Johnson had let them down. Democrats who wanted peace felt Hubert Humphrey would simply carry on Johnson's policies if elected President. Alabama Governor George Wallace lured millions of voters from both parties. The majority of Americans, used to winning wars, wanted the U.S. to drive the North Vietnamese out of Vietnam. They did not want a South Vietnamese government that shared power with the Viet Cong. When Richard Nixon hinted he had a

plan to end the war honorably, the public believed him; and he won the votes he needed.

The new President brought many fresh faces to Washington. Among them was a former Harvard instructor, Henry Kissinger. Kissinger had been a Kennedy adviser briefly but was unable to influence the people who surrounded John F. Kennedy. He became a friend of Nelson Rockefeller, who wanted to be the Republican Party candidate for President in 1968. When Republicans nominated Nixon instead, Kissinger let it be known that he wanted to help if Nixon became President. Shortly after the election, Nixon asked Kissinger to help him run the new President's National Security Council. Kissinger immediately took charge and began to grab power from Melvin Laird, Secretary of Defense, and William P. Rogers, Secretary of State.

A confident Richard M. Nixon during his successful bid for the presidency in 1968.

Secretary of Defense Melvin Laird introduced the idea of Vietnamization.

Kissinger was the kind of person who loved to be the center of attention. He often said funny or nasty things so that he would be quoted in the newspapers. He enjoyed manipulating people while influencing world events.

The first controversy involving Kissinger was the bombing of Cambodia,* which began in March 1969 at the urging of General Creighton Abrams. Kissinger convinced Nixon to conceal the operation. The decision to expand the war should have been shared with Congress. The bombing, named Operation Menu, was launched to punish enemy forces for increased activity in South Vietnam. For 14 months, B-52 bombers pounded suspected hideouts in Cambodia, whose border was only 50 miles west of Saigon. Nixon also wanted to resume bombing North Vietnam but decided against it. Such an action might have wrecked the Paris peace talks, where progress was slow.

Nixon saw himself as a great statesman. He believed he could convince the Soviet Union to pressure the North Vietnamese

*After the war, Cambodia was renamed Kampuchea. Since we deal with events before the end of the war, we use the name Cambodia throughout the book.

Henry Kissinger

Henry Kissinger (born May 27, 1923), former presidential adviser and Secretary of State

Kissinger fled the Nazis as a boy and became a U.S. citizen in 1943. He joined the Harvard University faculty as a professor and became a foe of world communism. The man with the slight German accent served the Kennedy administration and then worked for Republican presidential hopeful Nelson Rockefeller.

After Richard Nixon was elected in 1968, he asked Kissinger to be his adviser on national security. Kissinger accepted and then began to grab power from the military, from intelligence, and from William P. Rogers, the Secretary of State. In 1973, Kissinger replaced Rogers. In Nixon's view, the secretary was no longer needed.

Henry Kissinger did a number of controversial things while he served President Nixon. The most unlawful was to order the secret bombing of Cambodia, hidden from Congress and from the American people for almost four years. He also illegally wiretapped his own advisers when he thought they were telling the news media what went on in secret meetings.

When the Secretary of State won the Nobel Peace Prize in 1973, his critics were dismayed. They noted that he was being rewarded for helping to end a war he had supported! He also told voters just before the 1972 presidential election that peace was near. A few weeks later, he endorsed the heaviest air raids of the war over North Vietnam.

Kissinger also served President Gerald Ford as Secretary of State. In 1977, he left the government to resume teaching, lecturing, and writing.

into talking peace. His strategy failed; the Soviets either had no influence on the North Vietnamese or did nothing to intervene in the war. Kissinger knew that Hanoi would stall, talking peace as it continued to fight. Yet he still believed further talks were the only way to end the war, since the enemy seemed determined to fight on forever.

At about this time, President Nixon was handed a plan that Defense Secretary Melvin Laird called "Vietnamization." It simply meant that the U.S. would

World communist leaders attend the funeral ceremony for Ho Chi Minh, who died on September 3, 1969, at the age of 79.

slowly pull American combat forces out of South Vietnam, and Saigon would take over more of the fighting. The South Vietnamese would continue to receive U.S. weapons and aid, but American soldiers would gradually depart. Unfortunately, there was a major problem with this plan. The North Vietnamese could stop negotiating at the peace talks and wait until the U.S. pulled out. Then, they and the Viet Cong could wipe out the inefficient South Vietnamese.

Other problems faced Nixon and his cabinet. General Creighton Abrams, who didn't want to be blamed for losing the war, was requesting more, not fewer, American troops for Vietnam. In the United States, war protesters were staging demonstrations in towns all across America. They recruited new members to their side and tried to prove that the war was unpopular everywhere. Half a world away in Hanoi, Ho Chi Minh died of heart failure on September 3. In his will, he urged the North Vietnamese to continue the struggle. The will was read nationwide and united people who were already of one mind about unifying North and South Vietnam.

In the fall, Nixon appealed to "the silent majority" of Americans to back his version of how to end the war. He still had the support of a majority of U.S. citizens, but events were working against him. A group of Special Forces (Green Beret) officers in South Vietnam was accused of executing an unarmed prisoner. Other Green Beret troops soaked a Viet Cong flag in chicken blood and then sold it to pocket a few dollars. If elite troops were misbehaving, what were the draftees up to, Americans wondered. At the same time, the My Lai 4 massacre hit the front pages. The Phoenix plan, designed by the U.S. to assassinate suspected Viet Cong leaders, became public knowledge and shocked many Americans. No wonder the number of antiwar backers seemed larger with each demonstration.

Meanwhile, things were as bad as ever in South Vietnam. Urban areas continued to swell as rural people fled vicious fighting. In Saigon, Catholics, Buddhists, and others staged demonstrations against corruption in the government and the military. It was easy to see why corruption in South Vietnam was so widespread.

• American soldiers and civilians felt they had no future in Vietnam. So many people—from the Army's highest enlisted man to the lowliest warehouse guard—stole or helped the Vietnamese steal American goods to sell illegally in the cities. The black market, where stolen goods were sold, grew more active with each passing year.

• Some Vietnamese who were in power sent money, gold, and jewels out of the country for safekeeping, just in case they had to leave in a hurry.

• Censorship (preventing citizens from learning the news) was heavy in Saigon. News of the My Lai 4 massacre was kept out of Vietnamese daily newspapers, even though Americans all over Saigon were learning of the charges against Lieutenant William Calley. As a result, it was easy to keep reporters from printing stories about the corruption of government and military officials.

Morale, how a person feels about his status, was low among U.S. infantrymen, too. During heavy fighting in August 1969 south of Danang, a platoon refused to go further after suffering heavy casualties. The men, who were part of the 196th Light Infantry Brigade, were not punished for this refusal. Such confrontations between officers and their men were becoming more common as the war continued. In 1969 alone, there were 117 soldiers convicted of refusing to follow orders. In September, in the Mekong Delta, helicopter gunships accidentally killed 7 civilians and wounded 17 more. In an unrelated action, a helicopter crew killed 14 civilians by mistake in the village of Tamky.

Because the news seemed all bad, everyone from Vice President Spiro T. Agnew to the average member of the American Legion accused newspapers, radio, and television of having a negative point of view. Agnew echoed President Nixon's feelings by stating that the media was too liberal, antiwar, and as Agnew saw it, anti-American. Many Americans agreed with him. When a reporter asked a tough question of President Nixon at a press conference, readers, listeners, or viewers thought that the reporter was overstepping his authority.

Spiro T. Agnew

Spiro T. Agnew (born November 9, 1918), U.S. Vice President

Antiwar activists probably disliked Vice President Spiro T. Agnew the most of anyone in Nixon's administration. Agnew became Vice President in 1969 and quickly began to question the motives of those who disagreed with how the Nixon administration handled the war. He strongly criticized news reporters, opposing legislators, and antiwar groups, telling them that they were communists, fools, and "nattering nabobs of negativism."

Agnew's opinions reflected those of the President, Richard M. Nixon. The Vice President convinced many Americans that newspapers and radio and television stations were owned by a few "liberals" who didn't really like or respect the United States. He once went so far as to denounce fellow Republicans, simply because a group of them wanted "national reconciliation," or peace between disagreeing Americans.

It was fortunate that honesty was not a theme in Spiro Agnew's speeches. Investigators in Maryland discovered that Agnew had taken a bribe while he was the governor in that state. He resigned the vice presidency in disgrace in the fall of 1973.

Nixon and his supporters labeled the press a bunch of "wise guys" who delighted in making public officials and the military look bad.

The press didn't have to report one of the year's big stories in 1970, however; President Nixon made the announcement himself. He stated on April 30, 1970, that U.S. and South Vietnamese ground forces had invaded Cambodia. Not only was the action completely illegal (the President is required by law to consult Congress before invading a foreign country), the invasion accomplished little. Like many Nixon decisions, this one added fuel to the antiwar movement at a time when it seemed about to run out of gas.

At Kent State University in northeastern Ohio, students protested the invasion of Cambodia by attacking the Reserve Officers' Training Corps (ROTC) building. Ohio National Guardsmen killed 4 young people and wounded 11. The normally conservative National Student Association called for a nationwide strike on college campuses. A total of 100 colleges shut down, and students conducted strikes at 300 others.

More colleges closed as Congress received a flood of mail protesting U.S. troops in Cambodia. On the other side of the issue, construction and dockworkers staged a huge demonstration in New York City backing President Nixon. Vietnam was dividing the nation more and more deeply.

Nixon went on television in June to tell the country that the Cambodia campaign was a success. That was not true for several reasons. As soon as the allied soldiers moved west toward Cambodia, North Vietnamese began major attacks in northern South Vietnam. In Cambodia itself, allied soldiers failed to find the enemy. Instead, they discovered huts that had been empty for weeks and many frightened civilians. The civilians had good reason to be scared: The South Vietnamese, who would stay in Cambodia after the Americans pulled back, were traditional enemies of the Cambodians. Fighting between these two peoples resulted in many civilian casualties over the next few years.

These events should not be taken to mean that all South Vietnamese troops were cowards or criminals. Many units, particularly the Marines, fought bravely. Their casualty rates were always higher than those of American troops. U.S. advisors often left Vietnam with at least one story about how they and some Vietnamese cooks or truck drivers held off an enemy force after all the regular soldiers had been killed. It took courage for many of the 34,000 South Vietnamese troops to remain in Cambodia. They could be attacked by North Vietnamese, Viet Cong, Khmer Rouge, or Cambodian forces.

U.S. ground forces left Cambodia on June 30, 1970. That same day, the Senate voted 58-37 to pass the Cooper-Church Amendment. This piece of legislation was important because it cut off all military funds for a U.S. presence in Cambodia. It also marked the first time Congress had ever attempted to place limits on the President's powers as Commander in Chief of the military during a war. The more conservative House of Representatives voted down the amendment, but the warning was clear for the President. He would not be able to act as he pleased in conducting the war. White House insiders said Nixon's behavior became more and more unusual.

For example, Nixon usually spoke well in public even though he always used foul language among his friends. Now his every sentence seemed full of four-letter words and threats against people he saw as his enemies. In public and in private, he began to speak of himself not as "I" or "me" but as "the President," almost as if there were two different people in the Oval Office. He never viewed antiwar protesters as anything but show-offs and traitors. The urge to "get" his enemies would lead to the Watergate scandal and eventually to his resignation.

Meanwhile, there was no success to report in Paris. The North Vietnamese continued to insist that all American troops must leave Vietnam. If that happened, they said, U.S. prisoners of war would be released and no departing soldiers would be attacked. President Nixon refused. He then proposed that there be a "cease-fire in place" in all of Indochina. This would be followed by a peace conference with all sides repre-

A Kent State University student lies dead, shot by Ohio National Guard troops on May 4, 1970.

sented. North Vietnamese quickly rejected the proposal. Since American deaths were decreasing, however, U.S. negotiators felt less pressure to come up with a way to end all fighting quickly.

American "hawks" and "doves" alike continued to worry about American prisoners of war. The military decided to take dramatic action. On November 21, 1970, ten helicopters filled with U.S. volunteers flew across North Vietnam.

The task force surprised and killed the guards at a North Vietnamese prison camp believed to contain U.S. prisoners. The daring rescue proved fruitless. Once on the ground, the men found a completely empty prison. Due to poor intelligence information, the volunteers had landed in a camp that had not held an American prisoner for weeks. Luckily, the rescuers got out of the country without suffering any casualties.

Chapter 4

Border Wars

Especially sad chapters in the history of the war were written in Cambodia and Laos.

Cambodia, a neighbor to the west of South Vietnam, is no larger than the state of Oklahoma. There were never more than eight million Cambodians. Like the Vietnamese, Cambodians lived under French rule from the middle of the nineteenth century. They did not like the French, but they had even less regard for Vietnam and Thailand. Historically, Vietnamese and Thais had ruled all or part of Cambodia before the French arrived. During World War II, France crowned a Cambodian named Norodom Sihanouk king of the country at a time when Japanese troops were invading Southeast Asia. In 1953, the French departed and handed the country over to Sihanouk.

Sihanouk is one of the most amazing people of this century. He managed to keep a pleasant but powerless country neutral and at least partially free from 1941 to 1970. He did this by being deliberately unpredictable and eccentric. He made strange or offensive comments to important people, and he had a terrible temper. In the middle of a meeting, he might leave to make a movie or to play jazz tunes on his saxophone. Once, after South Vietnamese troops killed 100 Cambodian civilians, Sihanouk asked South Vietnam for a new bulldozer for each death! Friends and enemies alike admitted that the king was strange, intelligent, and fiercely protective of his hot, humid little country.

Sihanouk called himself prince. He loved to be with the average Cambodian. He sometimes told naughty jokes to villagers and made fun of Cambodians who had tried to educate themselves. Sihanouk's dislike of the country's tiny middle class caused

Downed pilots could be rescued from heavy jungle by a helicopter with a line.

some middle-class sons and daughters to search for other leaders. They ran off to join the small but growing Cambodian communist party in the jungle. Sihanouk's biggest problems, however, were to come from outside Cambodia.

North Vietnamese Army (NVA) and Viet Cong troops used Cambodia as a place to hide. At first, American and Vietnamese forces received instructions not to pursue the enemy into Cambodia. U.S. and South Vietnamese diplomats feared entering Cambodia because China might send troops to aid the NVA. Also, America's allies, already cool to U.S. involvement in Southeast Asia, could cause trouble in the United Nations. The growing number of antiwar groups in the United States would have yet another strong argument for American withdrawal from Vietnam.

The communists set up large, temporary camps in Cambodia where they could rest, treat their wounded, and prepare for future battles. Meanwhile, Sihanouk cut diplomatic relations with the U.S. in 1965. He believed that Americans were meeting secretly with

Cambodia tried to remain neutral in the war.

Cambodians who opposed his rule and who wanted to topple him and take over the country.

In 1966, the prince made a move that was anti-American and anti-South Vietnamese. He told the communists that they could use border areas as hiding places. Equally important, he allowed ships that supported the communists to land and unload war supplies at Cambodia's seaport. In response, the U.S. did two things: It filed a protest with the prince and began to send American and Vietnamese commandos into Cambodia to find out what the enemy was doing. These brave soldiers returned from their so-called "Daniel Boone" missions to report that there were, indeed, enemy camps just west of the border. America denied, then later admitted, once dropping bombs in neutral Cambodia some time during 1966.

During 1967 and 1968, many U.S. soldiers in western South Vietnam believed they also had been on secret operations inside Cambodia. It was difficult to tell where one country ended and the next began because border areas were wild, unmarked swamp or jungle. Also, the most accurate maps were old and written in French. American and South Vietnamese accusations that the Viet Cong were hiding in Cambodia were confirmed by Associated Press stories. Two daring reporters visited a VC camp, then described what they saw in a wire service story. Prince Sihanouk called it a lie. He also decided not to allow any more American journalists into Cambodia.

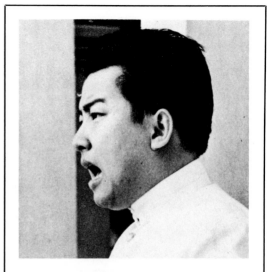

Norodom Sihanouk

Norodom Sihanouk (born October 31, 1922), former king, prime minister, and head of state of Cambodia

Sihanouk is a colorful, complex man who kept his small country free and independent for 15 years. Born to a Cambodian prince and princess, Sihanouk was named king at the age of 18 in 1941.

In 1955, after a series of defeats in Indochina, France pulled out of Cambodia. Sihanouk formed a political party and became prime minister.

He was overthrown in 1970 while visiting outside the country. Sihanouk blamed the United States for losing his throne. The U.S. appears to have backed Sihanouk's successor, Lon Nol.

Sihanouk returned to Cambodia after the Khmer Rouge took control in 1975. He found he liked mob rule no better than he had liked colonialism. Sihanouk called himself a roving ambassador for a while, then resigned and left the country to go overseas in 1976.

From his home in Beijing, China, he has continued to work for peace and independence in Cambodia.

U.S. B-52 bombers like this one saturated enemy-held jungles in Vietnam, Cambodia, and Laos throughout the war.

Little changed until after Richard Nixon was elected President in November 1968. Four months later, U.S. B-52 bombers pounded rural areas in Cambodia where NVA and Viet Cong troops were thought to be hiding. In part because the prince feared both the communists and the people who called themselves his friends, Sihanouk restored diplomatic ties with America in June 1969. Less than a year later, while Prince Sihanouk was out of the country, pro-American Cambodians seized control of the government. They may have acted in part because the prince was becoming more friendly with the leaders of North Vietnam.

At the same time *The New York Times* reported that American planes were bombing Cambodia (Nixon's Operation Menu). This was bigger news to most Americans than Sihanouk's overthrow; those who supported the war endorsed the bombing, while antiwar forces insisted on an immediate end to Operation Menu. There also were concerns that Nixon and Kissinger had violated the Constitution by trying to keep the bombings secret. Kissinger con-

vinced Nixon that *The New York Times* had been tipped off by a member of the President's staff. Even though it was illegal, Kissinger ordered wiretaps put on advisers' telephones to find out if someone was leaking White House decisions to reporters.

If secrecy was on Kissinger's mind, survival was on the minds of more and more Cambodians. The bombing had killed thousands of Cambodian village residents. The goal of the bombing was to destroy the one big enemy headquarters coordinating all activities aimed at defeating South Vietnamese and U.S. forces. The truth was, no such headquarters existed. As the bombs hammered away, the communists moved farther west into Cambodia. They were pursued for two months in 1970 by American and South Vietnamese troops in an invasion considered illegal by almost all countries. Cambodian citizens found themselves caught among American, Vietnamese, and Cambodian government troops and communist forces. It proved a bad place to be.

The Cambodian communists were called Khmer Rouge, a

Villagers often were tortured or killed by troops on both sides in the war.

French term meaning "Red Cambodians." As the fighting made it harder to earn a living, more Cambodians filled the ranks of the Khmer Rouge. These guerrillas were a rural force in a land with a rural population. Cambodians fought each other so fiercely that it sickened U.S. reporters. Soldiers on both sides cut off the heads of their enemies. Civilians, especially those of Vietnamese descent, were gunned down almost as if it were a sport. Children were taken into the armies, where they learned to kill with enthusiasm. European and American observers had always believed the Cambodians to be peaceful. Once the killing started, though, there seemed no end to it as thousands died.

The man who overthrew Prince Sihanouk was named Lon Nol. He was an army general whose health was poor. He continued to try to run the country after suffering a stroke, which occurred about the same time that North Vietnamese soldiers attacked some of his troops. All the while, the bombing continued until August 1973, when a cutoff in funds by the U.S. Congress forced a halt to the operation. Only a week before the B-52 flights ended, a U.S. bomb accidentally hit a Cambodian city, killing 125 innocent persons.

American air power sometimes hit civilian areas, such as this neighborhood in the North Vietnamese port city of Haiphong. This scene is typical of the destruction bombs brought to many cities throughout Indochina.

The following year, the Khmer Rouge surrounded and attacked many government positions. Except for the capital of Phnom Penh, major cities were in communist hands. The Khmer Rouge walked into a fearful Phnom Penh on April 17, 1975, just 13 days before Saigon was to fall to Vietnamese communists. The Khmer Rouge ordered foreigners out of their country and told Cambodians to leave the capital. They then began to kill almost everyone who was a member of the old government. The slaughter continued for several years. It is estimated that between two and four million Cambodians were killed. The true total will probably never be known.

If Cambodia was a somewhat backward nation, Laos, Vietnam's neighbor to the northwest, was even more so. About 3.5 million people lived in a mountainous land smaller than the state of Oregon. The country was a kingdom ruled by three different princes at the same time—one neutral, one communist, and one pro-western. During the Vietnam conflict, a secret war raged between America's Central Intelli-

A secret war was waged for years in Laos.

gence Agency (CIA) and the North Vietnamese. While the CIA taught Laotian tribes to resist communism, the North Vietnamese gave aid to Laotian communists, known as Pathet Lao. To complicate matters, much of the Ho Chi Minh Trail wound through Laos.

The trail was the target in 1971 of a large invasion of Laos by South Vietnamese. Thousands of troops, supported by American air

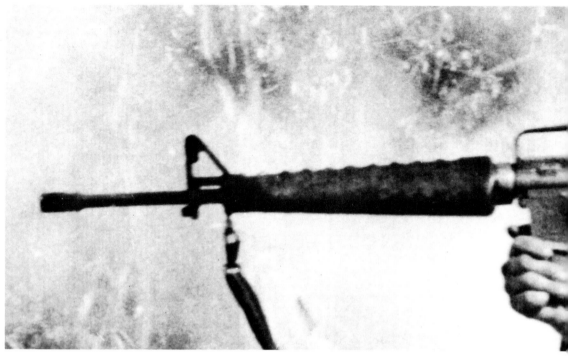

A Cambodian soldier tries to hold off the enemy in fighting near Phnom Penh in 1975.

power and equipment, moved into Laos in an attempt to cut the enemy supply line. U.S. bombs turned the landscape to dust, but the 30,000 South Vietnamese troops found it hard to move in the pockmarked jungle. A town on the trail, Tchepone, was captured by ARVN soldiers. But it had taken the South Vietnamese so long to reach the town that the enemy was long gone by the time they arrived.

The North Vietnamese were slow at first to defend against the invasion. They weren't sure what was happening, and they were led to believe that U.S. gunboats were making a landing in the north. The delay did not last long. As soon as South Vietnamese forces began to withdraw, the NVA attacked with a vengeance. They overran artillery bases when bad weather prevented American pilots from protecting the South Vietnamese withdrawal. The communists badly mauled several

Government troops had modern weapons but could not stop the rebel offensive.

different Vietnamese units, forcing the retreating soldiers to leave many wounded comrades behind. The wounded had no way to get out of these areas where U.S. B-52 high-altitude bombers would soon wipe them out. About 1,150 South Vietnamese, 100 Americans, and 13,000 NVA soldiers died during the ill-fated invasion into Laos.

Once again, Americans saw the drama on television in their living rooms. They watched as South Vietnamese soldiers desperately clung to the skids of helicopters to escape the jungle as North Vietnamese troops closed in. America's ally appeared to be taking heavy casualties. In fact, civilians and military alike suffered in Laos for 15 years, although fewer civilians were injured than in Vietnam or Cambodia. Many pro-western tribal people, however, were killed after the communist takeover in 1975 as they attempted to flee to Thailand.

U.S. helicopter crews provide covering fire for advancing Army of the Republic of Vietnam (ARVN) troops.

Two other groups also suffered greatly in Cambodia and Laos. They were U.S. military and civilian pilots and their crews. Army and CIA flyers alike encountered withering ground fire, especially along the Ho Chi Minh Trail in Laos. Many of the men whose names are among those missing in action were shot down over Cambodia or Laos. To this list must be added the missing pilots who were hit over North Vietnam and tried in vain to fly their damaged planes to Thailand. Laotian authorities agreed in 1985 to help the U.S. look for downed flyers. Few, if any, will return.

Throughout the war, acts of heroism in trying to find and rescue downed pilots were almost routine. One elite U.S. Air Force unit alone saved hundreds of pilots who had survived being shot down over hostile territory. Active in rescue operations all over Southeast Asia from 1962 to 1973, pararescue personnel saved 3,883 pilots and crews while losing 71 members and 45 of their own aircraft.

Chapter 5

Weapons of War

At the height of the war, both sides were using terrible—and terribly effective—weapons on each other. Many of the weapons were developed while fighting took place in Vietnam. As soldiers ran into problems, weapons were invented to solve those problems. Not all of the devices were made out of metal or explosives. Some weapons were instead psychological and worked on the opposing army's mind.

A weapon greatly feared by North Vietnamese and Viet Cong soldiers was the "beehive" artillery round. The beehive was an artillery shell with 8,000 nail-sized darts in it. Most artillery shells designed to stop foot soldiers contained steel balls or pellets. When the beehive was fired from a gun, the nose blew off, releasing the darts, which sounded like a swarm of bees zooming toward the enemy. The shells, first used in late 1966, were fired horizontally at close range. The rounds actually nailed enemy soldiers to trees or stuck their weapons and clothing to their bodies. Beehives were used by U.S. and South Vietnamese units when they caught the enemy in the open or when they were in danger of being overrun by human-wave attacks.

Artillery in various sizes could deliver shells more than 20 miles away. Different kinds of rounds did different jobs. A "HEAT" round was a "high-explosive anti-tank" shell. Since the enemy had few tanks, HEAT rounds were fired at bunkers and at buildings. "HE" and "HEP" stood for "high explosive" and "high-exlosive phosphorus." The phosphorus ignited on contact with the atmosphere and caused terrible burns.

Since the men firing the artillery could not see what they were trying to hit, forward observers ordered the kind of round to be

Rockets and miniguns make this Cobra helicopter a mobile platform for fire-power.

used and told the gunners where to aim. The troops at the artillery base used maps and mathematics to check the observers' requests. The Viet Cong had no real artillery, and the North Vietnamese Army had much less than did American or ARVN soldiers.

Artillery had major advantages and disadvantages. The biggest advantage was the ability to fire shells quickly at the enemy. Unlike airplanes, artillery worked well in any kind of weather. Americans and South Vietnamese often used artillery as "H & I" (harassment and interdiction) fire. A battery of four to six guns would fire off and on, around the clock, in an area where enemy soldiers were known to be. The shells kept the enemy constantly moving, awake, and afraid.

The disadvantages of artillery were numerous. It could not be used where enemy forces and friendly forces were close to each other. Shells didn't always land where they were aimed and could hit friendly forces. If the enemy was in thick jungle, artillery shells might explode in the treetops without doing much damage. Artillery was only as accurate as

the forward observers and the gunners. In addition, artillery fire bases had to be guarded constantly, since the enemy often tried to overrun them.

Many armored vehicles were little more than artillery pieces on tracks. The most commonly seen U.S. tank, the M48A3, had a 90-millimeter gun and carried about 50 shells and a four-man crew. Tanks were limited by the terrain; they were driven on roads but could not be used in Mekong Delta rice paddies or central highland jungles. The tracked vehicle used most in Vietnam was the M113 armored personnel carrier (APC). It carried a driver and a commander who manned the machine gun. This squat-looking box on treads could transport an infantry squad of eight to ten men. The APC served as an attack vehicle, an ambulance, and an ammunition hauler as well. The major disadvantage of the APC was its light weight. Even machine-gun bullets could pass straight through its light armor and kill the men inside. Mines and rockets easily disabled the vehicle.

New kinds of boats were needed in Vietnam. Called the

Six recoilless rifles can be seen on this U.S. Marine Ontos track vehicle.

"brown-water navy," these boats were either small patrol craft with automatic weapons, armored boats with everything from cannons to flame throwers, or troop carriers that ran across the water on cushions of air. Used along the coast and in the "oatmeal" of the Mekong Delta, the patrols proved highly effective.

River warfare in the delta was a complex operation. A huge troop ship carried soldiers to the mouth of a river. Infantrymen then left the ship on dozens of smaller craft. They roared into the delta in pursuit of the Viet Cong. Coastal duty included stopping any boats that might be carrying weapons or supplies to the enemy.

Weapons used by the Viet Cong and the NVA got more sophisticated as the war went on. The single most feared weapon used by the VC was the RPG7 rocket launcher. It fired a B-41 rocket with a shaped charge that exploded forward into anything it hit. Accurate for about one-quarter of a mile, the rockets (along with mortars) were regularly fired at U.S. bases. Two men could carry the launcher and several rockets. Moving around

Aluminum boats carrying 50-caliber machine guns and mortars were used by the U.S. and South Vietnamese to patrol miles of coastline.

North Vietnamese stand ready with an automatic weapon, awaiting U.S. planes over Hanoi.

the edge of a base, they could cause a great deal of injury and damage. In this respect, the rockets were even more effective than mortars, which took more time to set up and aim.

Both sides had rockets, guided by wires, that could be aimed by a soldier with a joystick after they were fired! When these curious weapons were launched, they left a trail of wire attached to the joystick. The rocket could be adjusted up, down, or sideways as it flew toward the target. Some of these small missiles flew so slowly that they could actually be seen and dodged. They were not much more accurate than the U.S. LAW (light antitank weapon), a rocket fired from a disposable fiberglass tube. There were also recoilless rifles, so called because these weapons produced a blast of fire out the back but produced no recoil or "kick."

The rocket tubes were light compared to the antiaircraft pieces used by the North Vietnamese. Some of these guns could fire miles into the air and had crews of five or more. Such guns were placed where U.S. aircraft were most likely to fly over. The jets

Over 6,000 rounds a minute erupt from an electrically driven gun aboard an AC-47 "Puff the Magic Dragon" plane. The aircraft were valuable in defending outposts under night attack. The pilot fired the mini-guns through a side-window sight.

moved at speeds of hundreds of miles an hour. So the North Vietnamese gunners, who might be laborers or farmers during non-emergencies, aimed at a point in front of the jet. They fired a barrage at that point and the jet flew into it. After the U.S. developed laser-guided or "smart" bombs to knock out the surface-to-air missiles, the antiaircraft guns were the most successful weapons used by the North Vietnamese to combat U.S. bombing raids.

No gun or rocket fired without sophisticated electronics could hit an aircraft at night. The U.S. had several highly effective planes that worked best in darkness. One was "Puff the Magic Dragon," also known as "Spooky." This aircraft was a slow-moving transport plane with electronically operated machine guns. The plane circled over a night-time battlefield, above a helicopter. When the helicopter drew ground fire, the transport replied with enough machine gun fire in one minute to riddle every square foot of an area the size of a football field.

A similar idea was the AC-130H Spectre, which operated at night over the Ho Chi Minh Trail.

Equipped with complex listening and "sniffing" devices, the plane could detect the noise or heat of a truck. Several automatic guns of different sizes then were fired at the enemy convoy. The plane also dropped homing devices for laser-guided missiles. Thousands of trucks were damaged beyond repair on paved portions of the trail through Laos.

Other American planes dropped psychological weapons on the enemy. Among the most common were small gifts or leaflets distributed by the millions. The leaflets told VC and NVA soldiers that they were on the losing side and that they should surrender under the "chieu hoi" or "open arms" program. An enemy soldier who did this was called a "hoi chanh." He (or she, in some cases) received money if a weapon also was given up. A hoi chanh was sent to a government school, then a job was found for him or her. Sly Vietnamese on both sides gave up, leaflet in hand, whenever they needed a rest from the war! They took part in the program, ate and slept well for awhile, then disappeared when the opportunity arose.

A few enemy Viet Cong soldiers joined U.S. forces as "Kit Carson" scouts. These were former enemy troops who knew the local landscape. More important, they knew where to look for booby traps and the kinds of booby traps manufactured in a particular area. These scouts frequently walked the point. That means they were the first friendly soldiers to walk into a dense jungle or a possibly hostile village. "I can't tell you how many times our Kit Carson scout saved us," says a former American infantryman. "I'd guess he's dead by now. I hope not, but I'm afraid he is."

One of the nonweapon items that would haunt soldiers on both sides was defoliation. The idea behind defoliants (chemicals that kill plants) was simple. If enemy soldiers hide in the jungle, then the jungle can be destroyed by defoliating. That will reveal the enemy without danger to Americans or South Vietnamese. Defoliation was one more example of good intentions that probably went wrong.

Agent Orange, the most popular defoliant, was first used in 1962. It was named after the orange canisters in which it was packaged. The liquid was sprayed out of planes flying over the thick vegetation. Made by the Dow Chemical Company and by Diamond Shamrock Company to military specifications, almost 20 million gallons were sprayed over Vietnam for 10 years. It killed the vegetation, but it did not turn up many Viet Cong.

There were other drawbacks to using defoliants. The substances killed all living plants, including rice, fruit trees, and whatever else a farmer happened to grow. One of the ingredients in Agent Orange is dioxin, a chemical thought to cause cancer and birth defects. Ground forces could do little except watch as cargo planes cruised above them, covering the landscape and themselves with a fine spray. "I was only 20 years old," said a former U.S. Army 4th Division infantryman. "It just never dawned on me that the stuff could hurt humans, too." Veterans blamed a number of subsequent physical and mental problems they suffered on their exposure to Agent Orange.

Both sides also used several kinds of smoke and gas. Ameri-

Agent Orange defoliant is sprayed above a South Vietnam jungle.

cans and their allies carried smoke grenades. These were used to hide soldiers who were being shot by a VC or NVA units. The smoke could be made in different colors. In a battle, an infantry unit could tell a helicopter pilot to fire a rocket west of the green smoke, for example. Tear gas was valuable, especially as a way to empty tunnels complexes. There were reports of poisonous gas used by North Vietnam against Montagnard civilians in the central highlands and in Laos.

Chapter 6

Shouldering the Burden

In theory, the policy of Vietnamization should have worked. The plan was to withdraw U.S. and other friendly troops so that South Vietnamese soldiers could do the fighting. That seemed to make sense. The South Vietnamese had one million men in the military—five times more than the combined forces of the Viet Cong and North Vietnamese in the South. Americans were willing to give the Vietnamese many weapons and vehicles so that President Nguyen Van Thieu and his people could continue the fight. But having more men and better equipment could not overcome other factors.

Big as it was, the Army of the Republic of Vietnam was not very professional. The entire armed forces operated on a series of bribes and payoffs. When a Vietnamese was drafted, he underwent training often given by a wealthy person who bribed some-

one so that he could become an instructor. Instructors never saw combat duty. As a result, they had no idea what combat was like. They weren't able to provide draftees with any knowledge about battle conditions or how to survive in the war.

Soldiers were paid only about $20 per month. At first, this was enough. But inflation (price increases) caused ARVN money to be worth less and less as the war went on. Since the people being drafted were young wage earners, their families often followed them wherever they went. It was not unusual to see a large ARVN column moving down a road, with their families strung out behind.

Other South Vietnamese forces known as the "Ruff-Puffs" were in even worse shape. These were Regional Forces (RF or "Ruffs") and Popular Forces (PF or "Puffs"). They were farmers and

"Merry Christmas Nixon, wish you were here" reads a sign at a Bob Hope Christmas Day show in Long Binh, South Vietnam, in 1971.

other laborers who had to work all day and then guard their villages at night. Stationed in rickety guard towers, these people were easy prey for Viet Cong in the dark. Their weapons wound up in enemy hands, and their deaths meant that the survivors would be on the road as refugees, headed toward one of the country's already overcrowded cities.

If the ARVN was in disarray, so was the U.S. military. In an unpopular war from the start, the military started out well but became less disciplined. No one wanted to get killed as fellow troops were withdrawing. Drugs were a terrible problem, so bad that in January 1971, General Creighton Abrams declared a separate war on drug use by American troops. Use of marijuana in particular had increased to the point where many soldiers were smoking the illegal substance while out looking for the enemy. Drugs also were used by noncommissioned officers — sergeants and specialists — and even by some junior officers. Soldiers who turned themselves in were treated and not punished.

There were visible signs that

Creighton W. Abrams

Creighton W. Abrams (1914-1974), U.S. Army general

Four-star General Creighton Abrams was named commander of the U.S. Military Assistance Command, Vietnam (MACV), in 1968. He replaced General William Westmoreland. A West Point graduate, Abrams was very different from the man he succeeded. He was short, used rough language, and had once been a tank commander. His mission in Vietnam was different as well. Instead of huge, dramatic operations, U.S. forces began carrying out operations with smaller groups of men.

As the war wound down, Abrams found he was able to do less and less with decreasing numbers of troops. He therefore strongly backed invading Cambodia and Laos, where he and others knew that the Viet Cong and North Vietnamese Army troops rested and hid their supplies. Later, as Army chief of staff, he successfully defended the role of his troops in this secret fighting.

After the last American combat soldier left Vietnam in 1973, Abrams supervised military aid to the South Vietnamese.

A Marine, soaked with his friend's blood, tries to comfort the wounded man.

indicated a unit's morale. If the men wore bandanas on their heads instead of steel headgear; if they slung machine gun ammunition across their chests as they had seen in movies; if they wore peace signs; if they wore huge mustaches or had long hair or seldom shaved; if they disobeyed orders—then morale was low. That meant the unit had no sense of mission and that the soldiers were more likely to be hurt or killed in a firefight.

Racial unrest in the ranks added to the military's woes. Blacks had noted earlier that a high number of minorities (people of Spanish, Black, or Asian origin) were in the field. In some combat units, as many as 25 percent of the soldiers were Black. The Defense Department took steps to make the percentage of Blacks and Latinos in combat more fair. But resentment between whites and Blacks grew. A white airborne sergeant, about to depart Vietnam early in 1971, was asked which candidate he planned to support in the 1972 presidential election. He replied, "George Wallace."

"He hates too many people," said a second soldier.

Presidential candidate George Wallace with his grandson.

"So do I," the sergeant replied.

As if there weren't enough military problems in Vietnam, a small group of antiwar military officers in the U.S. began a movement to hold war crimes trials against U.S. servicemen. The effort might better have been aimed at the South Vietnamese, who were well known for treating prisoners cruelly. For several years prior to 1971, persons who disagreed with the Saigon government were locked in tiny "tiger cages" on an offshore island. By the time Americans discovered this brutal treatment, many of the prisoners were crippled forever.

In April 1971 charges of war crimes against U.S. soldiers came from an organization that had first-hand knowledge—Vietnam Veterans Against the War. The VVAW staged a five-day demonstration in Washington, D.C. that attracted national attention. Tearful veterans, some of them war heroes, dumped ribbons, uniforms, boots, and souvenirs on the steps of the nation's Capitol and told of criminal actions they had witnessed. It was a dramatic moment, captured in photographs and on network newsfilm. The veterans later told a congressional committee that U.S. Marines had participated in the invasion of Laos. The invasion violated an earlier congressional action that prohibited Americans from fight-

More veterans spoke out against the war as it continued.

ing anywhere in Southeast Asia except Vietnam.

The U.S. soldier in the field learned about the deep divisions and discontent at home, though not through military channels.

Activist Buddhist monks protest government corruption in Saigon. They hold a painting

of a monk who burned himself to death to call attention to South Vietnam's problems.

Stars and Stripes, the daily military newspaper, was heavily censored. Numerous civilian editors were hired and fired as they pointed out they were not permitted to give soldiers all the news. Letters and magazines troops received from home indicated that support for Americans in Vietnam was weaker than ever. It was hard to think of the antiwar movement as small when 12,614 protesters were arrested in a single demonstration in May 1971 in Washington, D.C.

One of the results of low morale and poor discipline was that security around American bases in Vietnam became more lax. Enemy sappers (demolition experts) entered the U.S. air base near Camranh Bay and blew up 1.5 million gallons of aviation fuel. Firebases—remote artillery positions—became targets of repeated enemy attacks. Rolls of barbed wire surrounding the camps were not inspected each morning. This gave the enemy a chance to cut the wire on one night and have a clear path onto the base the following night. U.S. artillery gunners used more beehive rounds as they shot the dart-filled shells point blank at enemy soldiers charging through the wire in night or daylight human-wave attacks.

Throughout this period, the status of U.S. prisoners of war in North Vietnam was tied to America's withdrawal from Southeast Asia. The U.S. Senate voted 57-42 on June 22 for a complete U.S. pullout by June 1972. The only condition was agreement between America and the North Vietnamese on release of U.S. prisoners of war. The proposal was rejected later by the House of Representatives, but it shows that the Senate probably was more in agreement with public feeling than either the House or the President. In a press conference held the following month, relatives of war prisoners demanded withdrawal of U.S. troops in return for the release of their husbands, fathers, and brothers.

The last U.S. Marine fighting unit left Vietnam in July 1972. But combat continued. Over North Vietnam, American planes flew what Richard Nixon called "protective reaction" missions. In other words, when the United States felt its troops had been

A protester pretends to eat the rifle of a guard during a Washington antiwar rally.

attacked by the North Vietnamese, American planes flew northward, seeking to even the score. During the first six months of 1971, more than 40 such missions were carried out. On the ground, fighting was going on all over Indochina—in Laos, in Cambodia, and in South Vietnam.

In Saigon, matters were as confused as ever. Vice President Nguyen Cao Ky and another opponent of President Thieu announced that they were withdrawing from the upcoming presidential election. U.S. advisors pleaded with the two men to stay in the race to give it at least the appearance of being a democratic election. Both men refused. They claimed that Thieu had rigged the election and that nothing they did could make any difference. Buddhists, who were concerned with corruption, and Catholics, who were concerned about victory over the communists, protested the election vigorously. In some cases the protest took a violent turn. A terrorist bomb blew up in a Saigon nightclub, killing 15 people and injuring dozens more. Several groups claimed responsibility for the bombing.

President Thieu was re-elected in October 1971. He ran without opposition and won 94 percent of the vote. The election was not easy on anyone: Voters headed for the polls were attacked by Viet Cong in many villages.

If the ground war was winding

A paratrooper fights pain from a wound as he awaits evacuation. By the end of 1971, only 160,000 American combat troops remained in South Vietnam.

down for the Americans, the air war was as intense as ever. B-52 bombers, conveniently based in neighboring Thailand, stepped up their daily bombing of suspected North Vietnamese positions in Cambodia. Closer to the ground, American fighter-bombers and helicopters provided support for the South Vietnamese as they pursued the enemy westward into central Cambodia. Despite refusal by some U.S. forces to go into Cambodia, American advisors were seen with the South Vietnamese. This points up a problem in all wars for soldiers—Do they obey or disobey an order they know to be wrong? In no war was this question pondered more than in Vietnam.

Questions were raised, too, about how the war was conducted. At the end of 1971, American war planes staged several large, surprise attacks in North Vietnam as part of an operation called Linebacker I. They hit airfields, missile sites, antiaircraft guns, warehouses, and trucks. The White House provided reporters with a list of reasons why the U.S. was bombing the North Vietnamese so heavily. The primary reason was the continued activity of NVA units along the demilitarized zone and throughout South Vietnam. One reason not announced was that the U.S. had intelligence making bombing more urgent. They believed that NVA and Viet Cong forces would launch another Tet Offensive, this one at the end of January 1972. Could the South survive another such attack?

To head off the possibility, some ARVN units were withdrawn hurriedly from Cambodia. The pullout did their efforts in that country little good. But it did put many soldiers around Saigon, where communists seemed able to fire rockets whenever they pleased. South Vietnamese were being trained in the use of more modern weapons, then putting the weapons to quick use as the level of fighting rose.

No Tet Offensive occurred, however, despite an intense rocket attack on the big airbase at Danang. If there were to be a major attack in the near future, the Vietnamese would have to handle it. The number of American forces at the end of 1971 had dropped to 160,000.

Chapter 7

The North Rebuilds

The bombing of North Vietnam's cities stopped just before the 1968 U.S. presidential election. Gone were air raid sirens, the scream of jets, and the whistle and explosive fire of bombs. Gone, too, were many factories, roads, bridges, trucks, and other mechanical equipment. The bombing had set the emerging nation back several years. More aid was needed from Russia and China, since the bombs had greatly reduced production. For a time North Vietnamese leaders decided against escalating the fighting in the South. They chose instead to rebuild their shattered country.

Only Hanoi and Haiphong had buildings of any size still standing when the bombing halt came. Villages, never very well built, had simply disappeared in the bombardment. Frightened residents, who had been bombed because their village hid a gun or surface-to-air missile, lived in underground shelters. Conditions there were terrible. Sanitation did not exist and disease and snake and insect bites were common. If American pilots who were shot down reached the ground safely, they may sometimes have been torn apart by an angry mob.

How much punishment had the North absorbed? According to one of its leaders, in the summer of 1969 the country had been attacked 100,000 times by aircraft, ships, or artillery. American sources put the figures even higher. By late 1968, 107,700 air missions alone had been flown against the North, dropping about one million tons of bombs on the country. That's *three times* the amount dropped on Europe by the allies during all of World War II!

Few large industries were built or rebuilt. Instead, the North erected many small factories that produced bicycles, wire, cement, concrete block, tile, fabric, spices,

Hanoi residents prepare for air strikes by U.S. planes. The North rebuilt large areas during bombing halts.

sandals, nuts and bolts, tires, fertilizer, and more. Heavy and light weapons and ammunition came into the country in a steady stream from Russia and China. Private homes that had been destroyed in the bombing were rebuilt. The people laid rail lines once again, reconstructed bridges, and re-paved highways. For a while, it appeared that North Vietnam would become as normal as any undeveloped country could be that was still at war. The bombing had gained the U.S. very little in the way of a military victory, because North Vietnam produced very little. It was more like a big warehouse to store the materials and supplies coming from outside the country.

B-52 bombers continued to pound the Ho Chi Minh Trail and communist strongholds in Laos and Cambodia. In late 1971, photographs taken by U.S. Air Force planes showed heavy truck traffic moving south along the trail in Laos. Not only did the road have more pavement and other repairs, but also a number of anti-aircraft guns had been installed. These guns proved to be costly for American forces. Seven U.S.

planes were shot down over Laos on a single day in December 1971.

That same year, a diplomatic event occurred that alarmed and amazed North Vietnam. U.S. President Richard M. Nixon, for years an outspoken foe of world communism, announced that he would travel to mainland China. North Vietnam's huge and unpre-

A street in Hanoi is a mass of rubble following an air raid.

dictable neighbor was welcoming the enemy! To reduce Vietnamese fears, the Chinese promised more military aid. The Russians immediately increased their support, concerned that China was gaining more influence in Southeast Asia. Forty Soviet ships a month, most filled with oil and military supplies, were un-loaded in the North's largest port, Haiphong. Food and additional weapons and ammunition came into the country by rail from China. Hanoi concentrated on rebuilding the country, anticipating that relations with China might worsen and that Chinese aid soon might dwindle or even stop altogether.

No one wanted to be the last American to leave Vietnam.

Nixon arrived in Beijing, China, on February 21, 1972. He was welcomed in part because the Chinese had not gotten along well for some time with the Russians. The Soviets had massed forces along the border they shared with the Chinese. So China sought friendship with the only country on earth as strong, or stronger, than Russia. The North Vietnamese suspected that Nixon and the Chinese were plotting, behind the backs of their Vietnamese allies, to end the war. They wondered if they would be abandoned entirely by the Chinese.

With these thoughts on their minds, North Vietnamese leaders decided to increase the fighting in South Vietnam in 1972. Several reasons supported their decision. U.S. manpower was down to 140,000 men, the majority in non-combat roles. Russia had supplied North Vietnam and trained NVA soldiers to use new and improved artillery and tanks. Hanoi also considered South Vietnam more vulnerable to attack at this time. President Thieu's re-election had caused considerable discontent among the people, the South Vietnamese military was too commit-

President Richard M. Nixon's historic trip to China in 1972 greatly worried the North Vietnamese. Would the Chinese abandon their support of the North? they asked.

ted in Cambodia, and ARVN morale was, as usual, low.

The North unleashed an offensive on March 30, 1972. Long-range artillery thundered shells across the demilitarized zone, followed by thousands of troops led by 200 new Soviet tanks. The South Vietnamese and remaining U.S. troops did not know it, but this attack was the largest military operation since the Korean War. It made the 1968 Tet Offensive look small by comparison. Despite pinpoint artillery fire from American ships anchored just offshore, the South Vietnamese were pushed back steadily. Obviously, the North Vietnamese believed they could now beat their enemies in conventional battles rather than through guerrilla tactics.

Two North Vietnamese women form the crew of this antiaircraft position near Haiphong. The

The South Vietnamese made a stand at a key bridge. If they could either destroy the bridge or stop the North Vietnamese Army advance, much of the enemy offensive would grind to a halt. If they failed, NVA units would have little opposition between the bridge and the provincial capital of Quang Tri City or the old imperial capital of Hué. It soon became clear to Americans on the scene that the brave Vietnamese Marines with their few ARVN tanks would be overwhelmed. Two U.S. officers covered the bridge with putty-like plastic explosives, then made sure all Vietnamese were on the south side of the bridge. After several attempts, the electric charge ignited the explosives and the bridge collapsed.

North Vietnamese government had the overwhelming support of the people throughout the war.

North Vietnamese soldiers then swung west, toward another bridge. They were expecting more resistance, since there was a large ARVN base nearby. But two ARVN officers decided that a fight would only result in the deaths of their 2,000 men. So they and all of their soldiers surrendered to the NVA! The enemy also acquired several large U.S. artillery pieces during what was one of the most cowardly acts of the war. Shortly afterward, the NVA offensive was temporarily halted in tough fighting north of Quang Tri City.

But the offensive continued elsewhere. Far to the south, the NVA and its new Soviet tanks drove east out of Cambodia. Their objective was An Loc, a provincial capital. If they could take the city, they had a clear highway, through miles of rubber plantations, straight to Saigon. Even though American troops continued to leave Vietnam, massive air power was still available. Surrounded and inexperienced, the South Vietnamese nevertheless fought well. They were attacked by artillery but were protected by helicopters and jet fighter-bom-

bers. After weeks of close-in fighting, the enemy returned to Cambodia, defeated.

The North Vietnamese had long considered the central highlands the key to control of South Vietnam. In 1967, they had battered U.S. Marines at an isolated firebase named Dak To and then withdrawn. Five years later, they returned. The ARVN soldiers stationed there were attacked and overrun. Survivors straggled into the city of Kontum with the enemy not far behind. American advisors called in B-52 bombers, and South Vietnamese officers rallied their troops. The NVA repeatedly charged and were thrown back by tons of bombs. Their final assault, led by tanks, was stopped on May 27.

When all of this sacrifice was totaled, then added to the fighting in Laos and Cambodia, the courage of the average North Vietnamese soldier was incredible. Once he left home, at the age of 18 or 19, the chances of his ever returning were remote. Only those who were wounded or contracted malaria or other diseases were allowed to return home. The rest could count on little or no

Communist soldiers such as these had little to look forward to except hardship. Many who survived the war did so only because they caught malaria or were too badly wounded to keep fighting.

contact with their wives or families. One of the ways in which the NVA inspired such service was to portray themselves as part of a great historical moment. They believed that throwing out the Americans and their South Vietnamese puppets was the most important event in recent Vietnamese history.

The North also relied on several methods of controlling troops used earlier by China's Mao Zedong. Soldiers were divided into trios. These groups of three people would look after each other's welfare during a battle. Entire units worked as three-man teams. This method had several advantages. It helped soldiers get to know and care about two other key comrades. It boosted morale and gave the trio groups courage. And it made even the most quiet and withdrawn soldier feel as if he were never alone. American troops were constantly impressed by the courage of NVA and Viet Cong soldiers.

Equally courageous was North Vietnam's civilian population. Old men who had never been in an automobile were taught to fire antiaircraft guns at aircraft capable of speeds in excess of 1,000 miles an hour. Women who weighed 80 pounds worked from dawn to dusk to repair a bridge or a road or a dam hit by bombs. Today's young adults grew up without ever playing because as soon as they could walk they had jobs to do. Small children looked after babies. Larger children worked in the fields or tended animals. Many went to school, but school could be moved out of a city and into a forest if air strikes took place. Teenagers worked long hours in factories hidden in caves or underground. For as long as young people could remember, the country had been at war.

Recreation was sparse. There were government-controlled newspapers and radio stations but no television. News of the war—and everything else—was carefully managed. Once in a while, a war hero would visit a school or a factory. Or a troupe of actors would stage a battle where the NVA troops always won dramatically. But life at best was hard, and it could end quickly amidst the thunder that fell from above.

Women, children, and the elderly were expected to repair such damage, which occurred in an air raid on Hanoi.

Chapter 8

A Disillusioned America

By the end of the 1960s, there were few idealistic Americans left. The idealists had believed that a society of peace and love could be created and that the United States would be its birthplace. Citizens became cynical: They questioned the reasons fellow Americans acted as they did. An antiwar priest, for example, might be viewed by a cynic as someone who just wanted attention. Idealists turned cynical in the military, too. Many men who had thought of careers in uniform felt they had no support and became civilians as quickly as they could. People on both sides of the war issue had poor opinions of the government's actions. Was it out of touch, uncaring, or teetering toward a clumsy dictatorship?

The government was largely out of touch with what the nation wanted. Public opinion polls told what Americans thought or felt about an issue long before Con-gress acted on that issue. In the early 1970s, these polls showed that people thought the government did not do a good job of leading the country but instead lagged behind public opinion. This fact was evident in Paris, as well. Peace talks begun by Johnson had been going on for two years, yet they were talks in name only. Henry Kissinger insisted that the North Vietnamese withdraw from South Vietnam. Only then would U.S. forces leave. In turn, Le Duc Tho, head of the North Vietnamese peace delegation, said the U.S. must leave South Vietnam and stop supporting President Thieu. Unable to compromise, Kissinger and Le Duc Tho made no progress.

American soldiers continued to die in Vietnam, even though U.S. troops were withdrawn from Cambodia. Shrapnel (fragments from explosives) continued to be the most common battlefield in-

Many veterans believed that America was ignoring the problems they suffered as a result of the war in Indochina.

jury. It could injure or kill if a soldier tripped a mine or if he were following a fellow soldier too closely when a mine went off. Shrapnel came from artillery, from bombs, from rockets, or from hand grenades. These jagged bits of metal blew outward with such force that an explosion could level huts or trees or other vegetation. Wounds were usually dirty and therefore dangerous. As the war appeared to be ending for U.S. troops and civilians, they came to regard every wound as unnecessary. This attitude made soldiers more reluctant than ever to pursue combat with the enemy.

Antiwar and antigovernment protests flared throughout the summer of 1971. A commission appointed by President Richard Nixon reported that the country was as badly split as it had been during the Civil War. Americans were choosing sides, with poor people, Black people, and antiwar people on one side. They were opposed by many of the wealthy, much of the white middle class, and most conservatives. Nixon chose to delay the end of the war because he thought he could win "peace with honor." He handled

Le Duc Tho

Le Duc Tho (born 1911), North Vietnamese peace negotiator

Tho was one of a group of Vietnamese who founded the Indochinese Communist Party in 1930. Like his friend, Ho Chi Minh, he was imprisoned by the French for his attempts to bring independence to Vietnam.

When the U.S. arrived to prop up the South Vietnamese government, Tho went south where he helped organize political activities. In 1968, he became the chief negotiator for the North Vietnamese at the peace talks in Paris.

A clever man, he used the talks as one more battlefield in the fight for a unified Vietnam. Tho waited and waited for Henry Kissinger to give in on certain points. Eventually, he got his way in many areas. He refused the Nobel Peace Prize in 1973, pointing out that the fighting had not yet ended in the south.

people whom he thought were his enemies by sending Vice President Spiro Agnew out as a White House spokesman. Agnew called anyone who disagreed with Nixon names and threatened owners of radio and television stations if they did not report the news the way Nixon and Agnew saw it. Many Americans realized that Nixon was deepening the divisions in the country, and they were afraid of what the future might bring.

Meanwhile, neither the fighting nor the peace talks had brought more than a small number of U.S. war prisoners home. The few who had been released were turned over by the North Vietnamese to American antiwar groups. Throughout the war, Americans opposed to U.S. involvement found ways to visit Hanoi. The North Vietnamese permitted them into the country primarily for propaganda purposes. While some Americans opposed to the war provided the North with medicine and supplies, these items were unimportant compared to the appearance in Hanoi of an antiwar star such as Jane Fonda. The actress took an active

Jane Fonda

Jane Fonda (born December 21, 1937), actress and activist

Jane Fonda, the daughter of actor Henry Fonda, was a celebrity who joined the antiwar movement. She became as much a symbol of the peace movement as actor John Wayne became a symbol for the nation's "hawks."

Fonda did several things that annoyed the Johnson and Nixon administrations. She formed a group of entertainers who went to Vietnam as part of an antiwar show tour. She and others felt that comedian Bob Hope's optimistic military tours were not the only shows that soldiers should see. She also went to North Vietnam to inspect damage caused by U.S. bombs. Many persons concerned with the welfare of prisoners of war believed her actions somehow hurt their chances of early release.

As the war wound down, she married Tom Hayden, one of the founders of the Students for a Democratic Society (SDS). Since the war Fonda has won an Oscar and an Emmy for her dramatic performances. In 1987 she was named Number 1 heroine among American women. Her activism still annoys some veterans and other members of the public.

An American prisoner of war talks to fellow prisoners at a camp in Hanoi. U.S. prisoners were subjected to torture and other terrible conditions during their ordeals in North Vietnamese POW camps.

part in condemning U.S. bombing in 1972.

The public did not learn until much later that American prisoners of war, mostly downed pilots, had been tortured by the North Vietnamese. The northerners refused to allow much contact with prisoners or to obey the rules of the Geneva Convention. They considered the prisoners as little more than "pirates." How, North Vietnam asked, could they treat captives as war prisoners when no war had ever been declared between them and the U.S.?

Year after year, many Americans whose sons or husbands or fathers were listed as missing in action (MIA) clung to hope. Most MIAs were pilots or plane crewmen. In many cases, their fellow flyers were able to report back to the airbase or the ship that they saw parachutes appear as planes went down. In earlier wars, missing men were declared officially dead shortly after the war's end. In the case of Vietnam, the U.S. government has not declared any of the 2,500 MIAs dead. This is so survivors will continue to receive federal aid. MIAs remain America's most persistent reminder of a war gone wrong.

Senator George McGovern (center, both arms in air) ran unsuccessfully for President in 1972. He promised to end the war if elected.

How could the prisoners have come home earlier? The North Vietnamese believe to this day that the U.S. supported President Nguyen Van Thieu too long. If America had withdrawn before the South Vietnamese national election in 1971, the war would have ended, they say. But Washington was not prepared to abandon Thieu at this time.

There were others, however, who wanted to abandon Thieu. Many were in the Democratic Party, which had been taken over by young, liberal antiwar planners. Most backed the presidential candidacy of a World War II bomber pilot who was now trying to stop the fighting. He was U.S. Senator George McGovern.

As the 1972 presidential election neared, McGovern began to win Democratic primaries, though George Wallace continued to drain votes from both the Democrats and the Republicans. Unfortunately, the Alabama governor was shot at a Laurel, Maryland, political rally by a deranged man named Arthur Bremer and could not continue in the run for the presidency. Wallace backers either decided not to participate in the 1972 election, or they voted for Richard Nixon.

McGovern's campaign was riddled with problems from the start. Fighting among different groups had divided the party itself. By the time the Democrats got to the Miami convention in 1972, they were at each other's throats. Mayor Richard Daley of Chicago, who had unleashed police on demonstrators in 1968, was refused admission to the Miami meeting. Many long-time Democrats, such as labor leaders and southern voters, were scorned at the convention. They ended up voting for Nixon, too.

McGovern continued to campaign, but he faced a serious problem. Opinion polls indicated that most Americans wanted the war to end. But many of those same Americans told pollsters they were going to support Richard Nixon anyway, a man who had been unable to end the war in four years. It appears today that McGovern's backers lost him votes. They were too young (this was the first time 18-year-olds could vote) and too liberal. They

A bullet paralyzed George Wallace, ending his 1972 presidential campaign.

Democrats in 1972 prevented Chicago's Mayor Daley from taking part in their convention.

upset middle-aged and older Americans, who were becoming more concerned with law and order and the economic situation and less concerned about Vietnam. When McGovern's vice presidential running mate, Senator Thomas Eagleton, revealed that he had once received treatment for a nervous disorder, the race was all but lost.

By the time the Republicans gathered to nominate Nixon and Agnew for a second term, only 6,000 U.S. combat troops were still in Vietnam. There were, of course, thousands of mechanics, clerks, supply specialists, and advisors as well. They were needed to keep the 6,000 fighting men in the field and to teach the Vietnamese how to operate the vast supply line the Americans were turning over to them.

With a sometimes troubled candidate and a party in pieces, the Democrats were a complete contrast to the Republicans. For example, when President Nixon ordered the mining of North Vietnam's harbors on May 8, 1972, he received thousands of letters and telegrams supporting this warlike move. The support came from

U.S. soldiers patrol a coconut grove.

Though American casualties declined in the 1970s, Vietnamese civilians continued to die in terrible numbers.

107

Republicans around the country who had been told what to write. In the Democratic camp, labor unions and others were abandoning McGovern's sinking ship and saying so publically in newspapers and on radio and television.

Richard Nixon's only apparent problem was keeping the South Vietnamese from fouling up the withdrawal of U.S. forces. President Thieu had been openly critical of the U.S. ever since Henry Kissinger and the North Vietnamese began to meet secretly in Paris. The first secret meeting took place in 1970. Neither the Saigon government nor the Viet Cong were invited. Nixon assured Thieu that any future agreement would include the continued American protection of South Vietnam. Perhaps understandably, Thieu did not believe this message. On one hand Nixon was telling the American people that their boys had all but returned, while on the other he was assuring Thieu that U.S. support would go on forever.

Meanwhile, Henry Kissinger received revised versions of a peace treaty from North Vietnam's Le Duc Tho. It called for a

Nguyen Van Thieu.

cease-fire, an end to the war, release of all prisoners of war, and withdrawal of troops. The tough political questions would be settled between the South Vietnamese and the Viet Cong. Kissinger was delighted, since the peace offer came one month before the U.S. election in November 1972. Kissinger pre-

Henry Kissinger (far right) at the peace talks in Paris

sented the peace offer to Thieu on October 12. Thieu read the offer and soon believed that Kissinger had been tricked by the North Vietnamese. The South Vietnamese president and the U.S. diplomat quickly grew to hate each other. Thieu angrily denounced the agreement.

As the talks continued, North Vietnamese and Viet Cong soldiers quietly began to grab South Vietnamese territory. They wanted to be in control of as many villages as possible when peace came. Thieu and his forces became aware of this strategy and rounded up thousands of suspected communists. Thieu's action annoyed the North Viet-

U.S. Marines at Danang pack up and head for home.

namese to the point that they objected to treaty agreements they had reached earlier. To confuse matters even more, Kissinger announced to the American public that "peace is at hand" on October 31, just when it was falling apart. He was accused of trying to ensure that President Nixon would be re-elected in November.

Richard Nixon was indeed re-elected—by a record margin. Because he is an unusual person, the smashing victory over the Democrats didn't seem to make him happy. He brooded by the hour in the White House as he and Kissinger grew further apart. Kissinger had in the past made fun of the President among a few close friends. In December of 1972, Nixon seemed to be making fun of himself. He sent the North Vietnamese a threat that they would be sorry if they did not immediately return to the bargaining table! Nixon had said he wanted the North Vietnamese to think he was a "madman" and be frightened into making peace. While his actions seemed to confirm the idea, the North Vietnamese refused to back down on their demands.

Chapter 9

America Departs

Richard Nixon saw himself as an outsider. A strange and lonely man, we can only imagine what drove him to run repeatedly for public office. Once elected, he acted as if he didn't enjoy serving his term of office. Years before being President, he lost an election for governor of California. He felt the press had treated him badly and told them that "You won't have Richard Nixon to kick around any more." From mistrusting the news media to mistrusting almost everyone—that was one of Nixon's major problems as a politician.

Nixon's re-election in 1972 was never in doubt. So it is strange that he allowed some of his advisors to set up illegal wiretaps on his opponents' telephones and even to break into places where his "enemies" kept their secrets. When a man named Daniel Ellsberg released secret documents about the early stages of the war, White House burglars broke into the office of Ellsberg's psychiatrist. On June 17, 1972, five men were caught in the Washington, D.C., offices of the Democratic Party national headquarters. It was in an apartment complex named Watergate. By an odd series of events this apparently routine break-in was related to Vietnam and had shattering consequences for Nixon later on. At the time, however, Watergate had no immediate effect on the war; but it did symbolize the President's tormented state of mind.

By election day, 1972, the peace talks were unraveling. Nixon and Henry Kissinger warned President Thieu that newly elected members of the U.S. Senate were even more dovish than before. They would quickly decrease the amount of American aid being sent to the South Vietnamese. This argument failed to persuade Thieu. He was convinced that the

An infantryman flashes a peace sign before boarding a troop carrier for a flight back to the United States.

Richard M. Nixon

Richard M. Nixon (born January 9 1913), 37th President

Has a more complex man ever been elected to the presidency? Probably not. Nixon should have been the best President ever. While still a young man he served as Vice President under Dwight D. Eisenhower from 1953 to 1961. He had an opportunity to see how the presidency should work. Instead he was one of the most troubled Presidents, breaking the law when he felt like it and lying to or hiding facts from Congress and the American people.

Known as a longtime opponent of communism, Nixon became a lawyer, was elected to Congress, then ran for President in 1960 against John F. Kennedy. He barely lost this election. Nixon

ran for President again in 1968 and won, in part because the Democrats were so divided among themselves and in part because he hinted he had a secret plan to end the war. In fact, he had no plan.

In some ways, the challenge of Vietnam was as hard on Nixon as it had been on Lyndon Johnson. He was forced to keep talking about successes as he decreased the number of U.S. troops there. He also spread the war to Cambodia and Laos without the knowledge or consent of Congress. Had he not resigned in connection with the Watergate affair and other illegal actions, he might have been impeached for widening the Vietnam War.

It was Watergate that brought him down. He tried to cover up the connection between the illegal break-in at the Watergate apartment complex and members of his own staff. As evidence mounted against him, Nixon resigned in 1974 to avoid impeachment.

The former President has written six books, including one titled No More Vietnams.

terms agreed to by Kissinger and North Vietnam's Le Duc Tho would wipe out his government. Wording in the peace treaty would allow North Vietnamese soldiers to remain in the South. The North refused to remove its men. The talks stalled.

America replied with Operation Linebacker II. Linebacker I had been the intense bombing of North Vietnam in April 1972 designed to slow the North Viet-

Daniel Ellsberg's release of the Pentagon Papers made Americans even more wary of their government. Ellsberg was a Defense Department expert who lost faith in the war.

namese Army offensive in the South. Compared to the earlier operation, Linebacker II was massive. B-52 bombers for the first time in the war hit key military targets in and around Hanoi and the major seaport of Haiphong. The huge and slow-moving B-52s were now potential targets for surface-to-air missiles (SAM). To prevent new SAMs from being delivered, U.S. fighter-bombers once again mined the harbors. The North Vietnamese aimed every gun and missile skyward and alerted pilots of their Russian-made MiG jet fighters.

A total of 129 B-52 bombers—and two dozen F-111 fighter-bombers—pounded targets by night. Hundreds of carrier-based fighter-bombers and other Air Force jets hit military targets by day. The big bombers caused a great deal of destruction. Because B-52 bombing was precise, civilian casualties were not as great as most people feared. However, many Hanoi residents who lived near rail yards, airports, or warehouses were killed or injured. One wing of a hospital, next door to a runway, was hit by bombs that were released too soon, before the

The Watergate complex in Washington, D.C. A break-in at Democratic National Committee headquarters here led to the resignation of President Nixon.

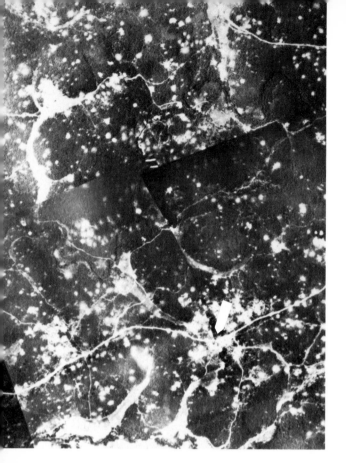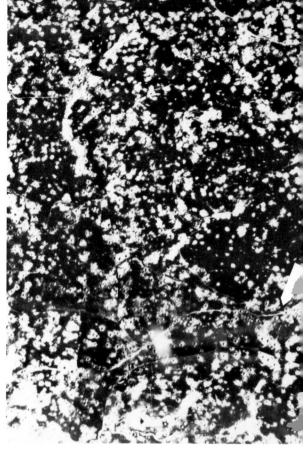

Arrows point to the same location before and after intense airstrikes in the demilitarized zone (DMZ) between North and South Vietnam. Craters are common in the left photo, but they are everywhere in the right photo. This is the result of carpet bombing.

plane had reached its target. The death toll from that strike was 18. Since each B-52 carried 20 tons of bombs, the North Vietnamese chose to save most of their SAM missiles for the night bombings.

The SAMs were not very effective against the big bombers. In fact, only one SAM out of 50 brought down a plane. Losses would have been even less but for one thing: B-52 pilots used the same route into and out of Hanoi for three nights in a row. On the third night, December 20, every gun and missile the North owned was aimed above the ridge of hills where the bombers first appeared. SAMs were fired in groups and detonated at different altitudes. Six B-52s plunged earthward and many others were damaged. Pilots and crews told their superiors that flying the same path, at the same altitude, night after night, was suicidal. The routes were changed

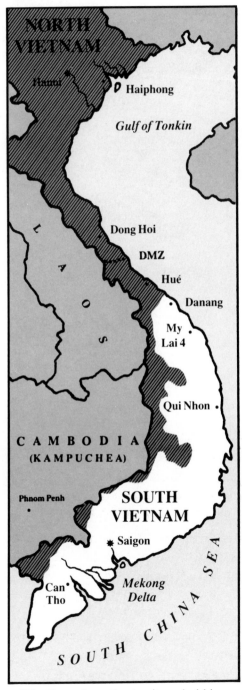

The lines show the territory held by the NVA at the cease fire.

after the December 20 losses to avoid such heavy casualties.

Despite a 36-hour pause for the Christmas holiday, the bombing was among the heaviest ever unleashed against any nation by another. Simply because they were in the vicinity, the Hanoi embassies of Cuba, Egypt, and India were damaged. Newsmen from all over the world were given tours of the city. They confirmed that "carpet bombing" (covering an area completely with bombs) had taken place. The North Vietnamese agreed to return to the conference table if the bombing stopped. They had fired all 1,200 of their SAM missiles and had lost so many MiG interceptors that most of the remaining ones were flown to airfields in China. The U.S. had run low on bombs and had hit all suitable targets. Several countries normally friendly to America, such as Belgium and Holland, protested the heavy bombardment. So did Pope Paul VI.

Linebacker II resulted in the deaths of more than 1,300 North Vietnamese. The U.S. lost a total of 26 planes and 93 pilots or crew members were killed, missing, or captured. Bombing of the demili-

tarized zone and other tense areas south of Hanoi and Haiphong continued until January 15, 1973. At that point, President Nixon called a halt and accepted Kissinger's January 9 announcement of a peace agreement with North Vietnam. (Kissinger had made peace announcements earlier that were premature.) Nevertheless, vicious ground fighting went on in Vietnam, where 4,300 more Americans died in 1972. The South Vietnamese and their enemies lost many times that number.

Papers confirming the peace agreement were signed in Paris on January 23. The cease-fire was to go into effect on January 28. The United States and the North Vietnamese had ironed out their differences, but each country had one overriding reason for agreeing to peace: America wanted out of the war almost any way possible, and the North knew that it could beat the South only if U.S. soldiers left the war.

At the time of the cease-fire the Saigon government controlled three-fourths of its territory and an estimated 85 percent of the population. Equally important,

the South Vietnamese were very well armed. America had left so many planes for them that they were the fourth largest air force on earth. With one million men in uniform (versus 150,000 NVA soldiers in the South), things looked optimistic for President Thieu. Sadly, four Americans died during the final week of war. The last was Lt. Col. William B. Nolde. He was killed instantly when an artillery shell hit his command post on January 27, less than 12 hours before the cease-fire went into effect.

The treaty contained several agreements that affected Americans. They included:

• Release of all U.S. prisoners of war within 60 days.

• Withdrawal of all U.S. troops and advisors within 60 days.

• Dismantling of American bases, also within 60 days.

There were a number of issues important to the two Vietnams. Both countries agreed to pull out of Cambodia and not return. Both said they would make the DMZ their temporary dividing line. Most important, any reunification of the country would have to take place, the agreement stated, "by

U.S. B-52 bombers dodged 1,200 surface-to-air missiles (SAM) during their bombing runs over North Vietnam in 1972.

North Vietnamese antiaircraft gunners

peaceful means." Both sides immediately disregarded this statement. Indeed, there were few signs in South Vietnam that the fighting was over.

The news of the peace treaty was received quietly in the U.S. Headlines and newscasts reported the story, but there were as many sighs of relief on January 27 as on January 28. Secretary of Defense Melvin Laird announced on the 27th an end to the military draft— taking young men into the armed forces. Students no longer had to worry that they would be pulled out of school and into a foxhole. Those who had had long-term commitments to the war, for or against it, now could make other plans for their lives. The Quakers who had peacefully walked a picket line for years in front of the White House departed. The scientists who had advised the military on top-secret projects looked around for different kinds of work. The families of the 57,702 Americans who died in Southeast Asia from 1965 to 1973 may have said prayers for both the living and the dead.

Timeline of Vietnam: 3000 B.C. to 1988

3000 B.C. The people we call the Vietnamese begin to migrate south out of China.

100 B.C. Start of China's 1,000-year rule of Vietnam.

A.D. 938 Vietnam becomes independent.

1500 The first European explorers visit Vietnam.

1640 Alexandre de Rhodes, a French Roman Catholic missionary, arrives in Vietnam.

1744 Vietnam expands into the Mekong Delta. The Vietnamese by this date rule over all of present-day Vietnam.

1844 The French fleet destroys Vietnam's navy.

1859 Saigon falls to the French.

1883 The French capture Hanoi.

1930 Ho Chi Minh starts the Indochinese Communist Party.

1939 The communist party is outlawed in Vietnam.

1941 The Japanese take control of Vietnam as Ho Chi Minh returns from a Chinese prison and the Viet Minh (communist army) is founded.

1945 Ho Chi Minh declares Vietnam independent as the Japanese surrender.

1946 The French return, and the Viet Minh take to the hills as the French Indochina war begins.

1952 Viet Minh forces are defeated several times by the French.

1954 The French are defeated at Dien Bien Phu and agree to leave Vietnam. Vietnam is divided into north and south following a cease-fire agreed upon in Geneva, Switzerland.

1955 The U.S. begins to send aid to South Vietnam.

1956 President Ngo Dinh Diem refuses to hold elections, as had been promised in the Geneva agreement.

1957 Communist guerrilla activities begin in South Vietnam.

1959 The North Vietnamese start to send soldiers into South Vietnam.

1963 The Viet Cong (South Vietnamese communists) defeat regular South Vietnamese soldiers at Ap Bac. This is the first major battle between the two sides. Buddhists protest South Vietnamese government policies. President Diem is overthrown and killed by the military.

1964 A North Vietnamese patrol boat attacks an American destroyer in the Gulf of Tonkin. Congress gives President Lyndon B. Johnson special powers to act in Southeast Asia. The first American pilot is shot down and taken prisoner by the North Vietnamese.

1965

1965 American air raids take place over North Vietnam. The first American combat troops arrive in South Vietnam.

February 7 Viet Cong attack U.S. bases. President Johnson replies to the attacks by bombing targets in North Vietnam.

March 8 The first American combat soldiers—3,500 Marines—arrive in Vietnam to guard Danang airbase.

March 24 Antiwar teach-in is held at the University of Michigan, Ann Arbor, Michigan. Teach-ins take place throughout 1965 on many college and university campuses.

April North Vietnamese prepare the first launching pad for Russian surface-to-air (SAM) missiles.

May 15 National antiwar teach-in held in Washington, D.C.

May 24 First U.S. Army division leaves U.S. for Vietnam.

June 11 Air Force General Nguyen Cao Ky takes over as South Vietnam's prime minister.

July 28 General William Westmoreland, commander of American forces in Vietnam, asks for and gets an increase in U.S. troops.

October through mid-November U.S. Army soldiers defeat North Vietnamese Army (NVA) troops in the first major battle between American and North Vietnamese forces. The fighting takes place in the remote Ia Drang valley.

December 25 U.S. bombing of North Vietnam is suspended by President Lyndon B. Johnson, who hopes the North Vietnamese will meet with him to talk peace.

December 31 U.S. troop strength in Vietnam numbers 200,000.

1966

January 31 President Johnson orders the bombing of North Vietnam to resume.

January-February The Senate Foreign Relations Committee questions President Johnson's advisors about U.S. involvement in the war.

February 8 President Johnson and South Vietnamese leaders call for peace following a meeting in Hawaii.

March 10 Buddhists demonstrate against the South Vietnamese government. Ky responds by using troops to quell demonstrations.

April 12 B-52 bombers are used for the first time in bombing raids against North Vietnam.

December North Vietnamese leaders meet and agree to fight the war with both troops and diplomacy.

1967

January North Vietnam says that the U.S. must stop its air raids before peace talks can begin.

January Operation Cedar Falls begins. This massive military action is designed to rid the Iron Triangle near Saigon of enemy soldiers. Villages believed sympathetic to the Viet Cong are levelled and the people relocated to refugee camps.

February 22 Operation Junction City begins. A plan to trap Viet Cong in a jungle area northwest of Saigon, the operation results in few VC captured despite five major battles.

April 28 General William Westmoreland addresses Congress on the war in Vietnam, asking for greater support.

July The North Vietnamese meet to plan a "Great Uprising" in 1968 in the south. The uprising became known as the Tet Offensive.

August Secretary of Defense Robert McNamara meets behind closed doors with U.S. senators. He informs them the saturation bombing of North Vietnam is not weakening the North Vietnamese.

September 3 General Nguyen Van Thieu is elected president of South Vietnam.

November U.S. Marines occupy Khe Sanh, a hilltop near the border of Laos. They are soon surrounded by over 35,000 NVA soldiers.

December 31 The number of U.S. troops in Vietnam reaches nearly 500,000.

1968

January 30-31 The Tet Offensive begins as Viet Cong and North Vietnamese troops attack most of the major cities in South Vietnam and the major American military bases.

February 24 U.S. and South Vietnamese forces, after weeks of fighting, retake Hué, ending the Tet Offensive.

March 10 *The New York Times* reports that General William Westmoreland wants 206,000 more American troops by the end of the year.

March 12 Eugene McCarthy, the antiwar U.S. senator from Minnesota, receives 40 percent of the Democratic vote in the New Hampshire primary.

March 16 Between 200 and 600 Vietnamese civilians are murdered by American troops in a village called My Lai 4.

March 31 President Lyndon B. Johnson orders a halt to the bombing of North Vietnam and announces that he will not run again for the presidency.

April 4 Dr. Martin Luther King, Jr., is shot to death in Memphis, Tennessee. Rioting erupts in many large U.S. cities.

May 11 Formal peace talks begin in Paris between the United States and North Vietnam.

June 6 U.S. Senator Robert Kennedy dies the day after he is shot in Los Angeles, California. Kennedy had been campaigning for the Democratic Presidential nomination.

June 10 General Creighton Abrams takes command of U.S. forces in Vietnam.

June 27 American troops leave Khe Sanh after several months of bitter fighting.

July 1 U.S. planes resume bombing north of the DMZ.

August 8 Richard M. Nixon is nominated by Republicans to run for the presidency.

August 26-29 Vice President Hubert Humphrey is nominated for the presidency in Chicago as police and antiwar demonstrators clash violently in the city's streets.

November 6 Richard M. Nixon is elected President.

December 31 A total of 540,000 Americans are in Vietnam.

1969

March 18 The secret bombing of Cambodia begins.

March 28 U.S. and ARVN troops discover mass graves of civilians killed by Viet Cong and NVA during the Tet takeover of Hué.

June 8 President Nixon announces that 25,000 American troops will be withdrawn, to be replaced by South Vietnamese forces.

September 3 Ho Chi Minh dies in Hanoi at the age of 79.

Fall Huge antiwar rallies take place in Washington, D.C.

November 16 The country learns of the My Lai 4 massacre.

December 31 The number of U.S. troops in South Vietnam drops to 480,000.

1970

February 20 Henry Kissinger and Le Duc Tho of North Vietnam meet secretly in Paris.

March 18 Prince Sihanouk of Cambodia is overthrown.

April 30 American and South Vietnamese forces invade Cambodia.

May 4 National Guardsmen kill 4 antiwar students and wound 11 others at Kent State University in Ohio.

December 31 The number of U.S. troops in Vietnam falls to 280,000.

1971

January 6 Congress repeals the Gulf of Tonkin Resolution.

February 8 South Vietnamese forces enter Laos in an attempt to cut the Ho Chi Minh trail.

March 29 Lieutenant William Calley is convicted of murder in connection with the massacre at My Lai 4.

December 31 U.S. forces now total 140,000.

1972

May 8 President Nixon mines the main North Vietnamese harbor and steps up the bombing.

June 17 A night watchman catches five men attempting to break into Democratic national headquarters at the Watergate apartment-hotel complex in Washington, D.C.

November 7 Richard Nixon is re-elected President.

December 31 U.S. combat troops number fewer than 30,000.

1973

January 27 An agreement is reached between the United States and North Vietnam to end the war in South Vietnam.

March 29 The last U.S. troops leave South Vietnam. The only Americans left behind are 8,500 civilians, plus embassy guards and a small number of soldiers in a defense office.

April 5 The U.S Senate votes 88-3 to forbid aid to North Vietnam without congressional approval.

August 15 The bombing of Cambodia by American planes ends. President Nixon criticizes Congress for ending the air war.

October 16 Henry Kissinger and Le Duc Tho are awarded the Nobel Peace Prize for ending the war in Indochina. Tho turns down the award because, as he points out, fighting continues.

1974

April 4 The U.S. House of Representatives rejects a White House proposal for more aid to South Vietnam.

August 9 Richard M. Nixon resigns as President of the United States and thus stops impeachment proceedings. Vice President Gerald Ford is sworn in as President.

1975

January 6 The province of Phuoc Long, only 60 miles north of Saigon, is captured by the communists.

March 14 President Nguyen Van Thieu decides to pull his troops out of the central highlands and northern provinces.

April 8 A huge U.S. cargo plane, loaded with Vietnamese orphans, crashes on takeoff near Saigon. More than 100 children die.

April 17 Cambodia falls to the Khmer Rouge (Cambodian communists).

April 30 Saigon falls to the communists.

December 3 Laos falls to the Pathet Lao (Laotian communists).

1976

July 2 The two Vietnams are officially reunified.

November 2 James Earl (Jimmy) Carter is elected President of the United States.

1977

January 21 President Carter pardons 10,000 draft evaders. Throughout the year more and more refugees (''boat people'') leave Vietnam by any means available. Many are ethnic Chinese who fear persecution from Vietnamese victors.

1978

December Vietnamese forces occupy Cambodia.

1979

February 17 China invades Vietnam and is in the country for three weeks.

November 24 The U.S General Accounting Office indicates that thousands of Vietnam veterans were exposed to the herbicide known as Agent Orange. The veterans claim they have suffered physical and psychological damage from the exposure.

1980

Summer Vietnamese army pursues Cambodians into Thailand.

November 4 Ronald Reagan is elected President of the United States.

1982

November 13 The Vietnam Veterans' Memorial is dedicated in Washington, D.C.

1984

May 7 Seven U.S. chemical companies agree to an out-of-court settlement with Vietnam veterans over manufacture of the herbicide Agent Orange. The settlement is for $180 million.

July 15 Major fighting breaks out along the Vietnam-China border.

1986

December Vietnam's aging leaders step down after failing to improve the economy.

1988

June Vietnamese troops begin to withdraw from Cambodia.

Ho Chi Minh.

Glossary

The glossary of each book in this series introduces various Vietnamese and American terms used throughout the war.

Agent Orange: A toxic chemical used to clear foliage from jungle areas. (See also definition for Defoiliant.)

Beehive: An artillery round filled with tiny metal darts. The round was used by the U.S. against enemy units.

Claymore mine: A small, curved plastic box filled with explosives and with 700 bits of steel. It looked somewhat like an old Polaroid camera, and it had a range of 250 feet.

Corps areas: American forces divided South Vietnam into four corps. I Corps was the area just south of the demilitarized zone; II Corps included the central highlands; III Corps was Saigon and surrounding area; IV Corps was the Mekong Delta.

Defoliant: Chemical used by the U.S. to destroy parts of the Vietnamese jungle so the enemy could be seen. Some veterans believe that defoliants like Agent Orange also harmed military personnel who handled the chemicals or were accidentally sprayed.

Khmer Rouge: Cambodian communists. The phrase is French and means "Red Cambodians."

MACV: Military Assistance Command, Vietnam. This U.S. military group had command over all military activities by Americans in South Vietnam.

Pathet Lao: Laotian communists. These people were aided by North Vietnam and led by Prince Souphanouvang.

RF-PF or "Ruff-Puff": South Vietnamese Regional Forces and Popular Forces. The RFs were civilians trained to defend their province (state), while the PFs defended their village.

"Smart" bombs: Laser-guided bombs that allow a pilot to aim the bombs after they are released from beneath the wing of a plane. They were used by the U.S. on important North Vietnamese military targets.

Vietnamization: A U.S. policy that involved the gradual withdrawal of U.S. and other friendly forces from South Vietnam, while the South Vietnamese Army took over more and more of the fighting. The word was first used by Melvin Laird, Secretary of Defense under President Richard M. Nixon.

Military police and protesters on the steps of the Pentagon in Washington, D.C.

Index

U.S. 1st Division troops in an old rubber plantation.

M

Mao Zedong, 95
Marines, U. S., 16-18
McCarthy, Eugene J., 15-16,
20
biography, 15
McGovern, George, 104-105,
107
McNamara, Robert, 14
Medina, Ernest, 29, 32, 34
Mekong Delta, 64, 66
Miami, 105
**Military Assistance
Command, Vietnam
(MACV),** 12
military draft, 123
minorities, in U. S. military,
78
missing in action (MIA), 61,
103
morale problems, 43-44, 76,
78
My Lai 4, 26-36, 43

N

**National Student
Association,** 45
Nguyen Cao Ky, 83
Nguyen Van Thieu, 74, 83, 90,
98, 104, 108-109, 113, 121
Nixon, Richard M., 19, 22,
25, 39-47 54, 82, 88, 90,
100-101, 105, 107-108,
111, 113-114, 121
biography of, 114
Nolde, William B., 121
North Vietnam
air bombardment of, 16-
17, 82-83, 85, 87-88, 96,
114, 116, 118-119, 121
civilians in, 87, 95-96, 116,
118, 119, 121
peace talks with U. S., 108-
109, 111
peace treaty with U. S.,
121, 123
rebuilding of, 87-96
**North Vietnamese Army
(NVA),** 12, 15, 16-18, 50,
58-59, 63-64, 66, 71, 73,
90-95, 114, 116

O

Operation Linebacker I, 85,
114, 116
Operation Linebacker II,
114, 116, 118-119, 121
Operation Menu, 40, 54

P

Paris peace agreement, 114,
121, 123
Paris peace talks, 23, 40, 46-
47, 98, 108-109, 111, 113-
114, 121, 123
Pathet Lao, 57
Phnom Penh, Cambodia, 57
Phoenix plan, 43
pilots, in U. S. military, 61,
103, 118, 119, 121
Popular Forces (PFs or
Puffs), 74, 76
**presidential election, United
States**
of 1968, 15-16, 19-22
of 1972, 104-105, 107-108,
111
**presidential election, South
Vietnam,** 83

Thousands listen to antiwar speeches in front of the Capitol in Washington, D.C., in 1971.

An amputee pauses in front of the Vietnam War Memorial, completed in 1982 to honor America's 2.7 million veterans of the war in Indochina.

Acknowledgments

The series *War in Vietnam* is the product of many talented and dedicated people. Their stories, experiences, and skills helped make this series a unique contribution to our knowledge of the Vietnam era.

Author David K. Wright would like to thank the following people for their assistance: Yen Do, former Saigon resident and now a newspaper publisher in California; David Doyle, who works with resettled Hmong people from Laos; John Kuehl and Don Luce, both employees of Asia Resource Center in Washington, D. C.; Patricia (Kit) Norland of the Indochina Project in Washington, D. C.; John Stolting, 9th Infantry Division, Awards and Decorations section; and Frank Tatu, Don Ehlke, and Donald Wright, all veterans of the Vietnam War. These individuals gave generously of their time in personal interviews and provided resources on Southeast Asian history and current conditions.

A special thanks to Frank Burdick, Professor of History at State University College in Cortland, New York. Professor Burdick reviewed the manuscripts and made many valuable suggestions to improve them.

The editorial staff at Childrens Press who produced the four books of this series include Fran Dyra, Vice President, Editorial; Margrit Fiddle, Creative Director; L. Sue Baugh, Project Editor; Judy Feldman, Photo Editor; and Pat Stahl and Norman Zuefle, Editorial Proofreaders. Charles Hills of New Horizons & Associates created the dramatic book design for the series.

Picture Acknowledgments

The Bettmann Archive—10, 11, 15, 23, 41, 51, 56, 58-59, 68, 75, 77, 79, 80-81, 88-89, 92-93, 106, 109, 110-111, 112, 120, 140-141

Black Stars:

© Mallory Hope Ferrell—Front Cover

© Tony Aviran—Back Cover

© James Pickerell—2-3, 31, 133

© L. Caparros—4-5

© Dennis Brack—9, 20, 21, 83

© Robert Ellison—17, 27

© Mike Abramson—24-25

© Bill Strode—37

© Stern/Scheler—38

© Howard Ruffner—47

© Owen—49, 70, 73, 118

© Russ Melcher—55

© Steve Northup—78, 105

© Lee Lockwood—86, 96-97

© Stem Clv Photo—95

© Connie Hwang—99

© Robert Davis—115

© Vietnam News Agency—122-123

Wide World Photos, Inc.—8, 13, 14, 18, 19, 22, 29, 30, 32, 33, 34, 35, 40, 42, 44, 52-53, 60-61, 62, 65, 66-67, 76, 84, 90, 91, 100, 101, 102-103, 104, 105, 107, 108, 114, 116-117, 131, 135, 139

Maps—Southeast Asia; note DMZ, My Lai, Saigon, Hanoi—28, 50, 57, 119

About the Author

David K. Wright is a freelance writer who lives in Wisconsin. He grew up in and around Richmond, Indiana, and graduated from Wittenberg University in Springfield, Ohio, in 1966.

Wright received his draft notice the day after he graduated from college. He was inducted in September 1966 and arrived in Vietnam at Bien Hoa in March 1967. He served in the U.S. Army 9th Infantry Division as an armor crewman. Wright was stationed at Camp Bearcat, east of Saigon, and at Dong Tam in the Mekong Delta. He returned from Vietnam in March 1968 and was honorably discharged in September of that year, having attained the rank of Specialist five.

This is the third in a series of four books by Wright for Childrens Press about the Vietnam War. He also has written a book on Vietnam and a book on Malaysia in the *Enchantment of the World* series also published by Childrens Press.